# Téa de León

Book Two of the *Not Here To Stay* series.

By Carolina P. McMullen

Copyright © 2015 by Carolina P. McMullen

All rights reserved. No part of this publication may be reproduced, distributed or transmitted in any form or by any means, including photocopying, recording, or other electronic or mechanical methods, without the prior written permission of the publisher, except in the case of brief quotations embodied in critical reviews and certain other noncommercial uses permitted by copyright law. For permission requests, write to the publisher, addressed "Attention: Permissions Coordinator," at the address below.
Three Bird Press
1121 Park West Blvd Suite B # 125
Mt. Pleasant, SC 29466

Publisher's Note: This is a work of fiction. Names, characters, places, and incidents are a product of the author's imagination. Locales and public names are sometimes used for atmospheric purposes. Any resemblance to actual people, living or dead, or to businesses, companies, events, institutions, or locales is completely coincidental. Book Layout ©2015 BookDesignTemplates.com

Ordering Information:
Quantity sales. Special discounts are available on quantity purchases by corporations, associations, and others. For details, contact the "Special Sales Department" at the address above.

Téa de León: a novel/ Carolina P. McMullen. -- 1st ed.
ISBN-13-9780692407134    ISBN-10-0692407138
Editing by Lorin Tinder
Cover design by Betts Keating
www.carolinapmcmullen.com

To my daughter.

*Even a child is known by his actions, by whether his conduct is pure and right.*
　　　　　　　　　　　　　Proverbs 20:11

## CHAPTER ONE

I was not at the little kids dance. I was at the teen dance, and boy was I happy to be there enjoying it with clandestine pleasure. Unfortunately, the fun was over way too soon. I felt my brother pulling on my white sweater until he got me off the dance floor. "Téa, you're in so much trouble! Dad knows you're here, and he's fuming, you better run home."

My father, Antonio, loved me very much, but he was also terribly strict. I knew my father's rules, and yet I deliberately disobeyed them.

I knew my father didn't allow my sister or me to dance with boys, especially me, because I was the youngest. As a matter of fact, I was practically the youngest of my seven siblings. My little brother, Nano, was the eighth and final baby. My sister, Lola, was the second born. It wasn't fair that she had been allowed to have a boyfriend ever since she was my age. Unfortunately, they've been together so long now that they are soon to be engaged. I hate his guts.

    I ran as fast as my legs could carry me, with my brother leading the way. I fell trying to catch up to him. He stopped when he heard my cry. "Téa come on."

    "I can't; it hurts." Antonio was my oldest brother, the first born. He looked identical to our father. My dear Antonio carried me the rest of the way home, but dropped me at the front door. It was up to me to face the wrath of my infuriated father...alone. Antonio stayed outside with his ear glued to the thick wooden door. As for father, he was tired of waiting. He had been waiting too long, and his eyes were hell red; the knuckles of his right hand were bleeding from hitting the wall in frustration and anger. From my father's left hand, a pair of scissors swung menacingly.

    "How many times have I told you not to leave the little kids dance? Yet you disobey me! How do I make myself clear? I forbid you from attending the teen's dance! Young lady, I'm about to teach you a lesson you'll never forget!"

"Papa? What are you doing? Please Papa, you can't be serious! Papa, you're scaring me. Please Papa, not my hair!" I cried as he grabbed my braided blonde hair. I had beautiful long locks that had never been cut in my whole life. He held me by one of my braids as I tried to escape. Running only made it easier for him to snip the hair like a piece of rope.

"Papa, no!" Father was running after me with his scissors like a madman. The chase around the kitchen table didn't last long, and Father soon had me by the other braid. He sat me on a chair and if I tried to rise, he would pull me down with one harsh yank of my remaining braid. Finally, exhausted, I gave in, and Father snipped his scissors like an unskilled shepherd, making holes as big as craters scattered all over my small head. My brother Antonio, worried for my safety, finally rushed through the door and in a single leap grabbed father. It was too late, I was unrecognizable. My pale scalp was bloody with cuts and bruises. I resembled the ghost of a child lost in a Nazi concentration camp.

"Father, stop! Father, in the name of God! What have you done?" Antonio was on the floor trying to restrain our father.

"Oh! Dear Lord, what have I done to my baby?" Papa began to weep uncontrollably. "Oh my baby girl, what have I done? Oh, please forgive me!" Father wept for weeks after that. He never forgave himself. And I, I will never forgive myself either. If only I had behaved, then none of this would have happened.

During the entire incident my mother was right there suffering with me, but knew better than to interfere with my father's method of 'discipline', no matter how cruel or harsh it might end up being. It was in the calm after the storm that my mother let her voice be heard, and did she ever do a good job. She made sure to scold my father every time she thought it necessary, bringing up memories of that awful day. Memories that were already haunting him.

My short hair, once white blonde, grew back quite slowly. Nothing grows slower than a bad haircut, or rather, a bad shear. My hair was never the same after the brush with my father's scissors. Not only did it grow back with a different luster, it was also darker, an auburn color. Me, who used to spend hours in front of anything that gave a reflection, now avoided mirrors like the plague. My dear brother Antonio covered the few mirrors that were in the house to spare me the embarrassment in case I accidently happened to look. I appreciated the gesture.

We were a family of farmers, and my father was pleased that six of his eight offspring were boys. The perfect combination, six boys to work the fields and two girls to help mother with the cooking and the many chores around the house. My mother, who was a saint, left the hardest chores for herself. She washed clothes in a barrel, scrubbing until the dirt and stains were gone from the garments. Her hands were haggard from the cold water and harsh detergents. They didn't match her soft face. My sister Lola tried to take over many times, as she loved my mother dearly, but mother would refuse her help telling her between huffs and puffs that she needed to preserve her hands for her wedding.

My brother Nano was the youngest and not strong enough to work in the fields yet. As for me, I helped with any little chore my mother or sister asked of me, but since my father cut my hair; they pretty much left me alone out of pity. In reality, I think they just couldn't bear looking at me.

It was April, and during that month it rained often, almost every day. With the rain came the moist fields, which brought snails and escargot into season. My mother would dress my brother and me in waterproof clothing and rain boots to keep us dry. Each of us would carry a large cloth bag with a few pieces of stale bread in it to keep the little creatures occupied. Of course that gave us the perfect excuse to spend those days doing more than just searching for snails. We loved to make the snails race. We would play for hours, since each race would take quite a while. I got very good at recognizing a good snail athlete when I saw one, making me the winner each and every time. As the day progressed, our tummies would rumble, alerting us to the time. Lucky for us we had plenty of food growing right there on our trees. Figs, pears, oranges and almond trees. Best of all, the biggest cherry tree I had ever seen in my short life.

    My father planted the cherry tree close to the water tank that he used for the irrigation system. With the passing of time, the small tree had grown quite massive, producing the best tasting cherries my lucky palate had ever sampled. My brother and I would sit on the rim of the tank, with our feet in the fresh water, splashing and laughing. We'd wash the cherries, and after a brief shake, consume the tasty treats. I remember most vividly the happy smiles my little brother gave me, and I can only assume my face gave him the same in return.

    Mother's voice echoed through the hills as we followed it back to her. She shook her head with a smile at the sight of our half-full bags; bags that should have been overflowing with slimy snails.

The tiny captives would spend a few days in a large bowl covered with a fine cheese cloth net to prevent them from escaping over the wall. This was where they would fast for a couple of days to rid their bodies of dirt and the like. The fasting would be followed by a diet of select aromatic plants. Before cooking they would be washed thoroughly several times with plenty of fresh water, salt and vinegar. When mother didn't see any slime floating on the water, she would cook them in a delicious broth infused with many spices. The aroma made my mouth salivate more than a snail made slime. I couldn't wait to put my hands around the first steaming bowl of the succulent dish. It had always been one of my favorite meals. My mother's talented gift as a cook kept me from getting too attached to the little creatures.

## CHAPTER TWO

# Old Versus New

The morning sun snuck in through the small cracks of the wooden roller shades making Téa's eyelids flicker. Yawning and rubbing her eyes, she walked out of the room that she shared with her brother, Nano. The house was quiet. Everyone else had risen and left before dawn. Téa knew her father and brothers were in the fields, but her mother was not in the kitchen, which was the first place she went looking for breakfast. She quickly took the opportunity to raid the pantry. That's where her mother kept the sweets, on the highest shelf, safe from the house pest; Téa. She had to use a chair to reach the goods. Pulling one over from the kitchen table, the girl determinedly climbed up on it. That's when she saw it sitting there all white and shiny, an extra-large can of *La Lechera*, the condensed milk Téa's mother used to sweeten her coffee. The little thief prayed to God it would be open, and it was.

Her eyes were moved to tears, as her mouth watered. She promised herself that she would only have a few sips. Without hesitation, the mischievous girl grabbed the heavy can, which was bigger than her face, turned it up and patiently waited for the thick white cream to hit her tongue. When she finally felt the heavenly cream touch her tongue, she couldn't help but to moan. Téa glued her mouth to the can and sucked down the milk like a calf sucking the colostrum from its mother's udders. As she enjoyed the rich substance, unconsciously, Téa broke her promise.

"What are you doing?" her brother Nano asked, breaking the spell.

"Uh? Nothing." Téa whispered after she licked the milk that was dripping down the side of her face. She returned the now much lighter can back in its place. "Come on, let's look for Mother," Téa said, grabbing him by the shoulders and pushing him out of the kitchen. Téa suddenly froze half-way, remembering that she had forgotten to take the chair out of the pantry. After removing any trace of herself from the crime scene, she quickly joined her little brother outside. She stepped outside barefoot and felt the warmth of the blonde silky sand.

The sun shone while grey clouds scudded along, and the morning breeze softly swung the white sheets her mother was hanging out to dry over the clotheslines. Téa's older sister, Lola, helped her mother by holding the pin basket. Nano placed himself underneath the sheets and played with a few fallen wooden clothespins making a choo-choo train.

When Mother was finished hanging the last of the sheets, she pulled her son's arm and in one hop swept him off the ground and onto her hips. Nano was very small for his age and still enjoyed clinging onto her like a baby koala.

"Breakfast time!" Mother sang. "Lola we need to keep an eye on these sheets; I smell rain." Nano still had a clothespin in his hand and was pinching mother's hair with it. He shared a naughty smile, amazed his mother didn't feel a thing.

Mother instructed Lola to put some stale bread into a bowl for a migote, and Téa's heart sank with fear as she watched her mother walk towards the pantry. Téa dared not look, but was relieved when she heard her mother shaking a bag of coffee beans with one hand and holding the hand mill securely in her other. She placed both on the table while Lola placed a pot of water on the fire. Téa loved to grind the little mill and asked her mother to let her do it. Mother nodded with a smile. It was always harder to roll the handle in the beginning while the beans were still intact. Lola, who was always in a hurry, unsuccessfully tried to take over. Mother stopped her older daughter with a disapproving look, and with a soft touch placed her hand over the younger's hand helping her with the first couple of turns. Slowly the handle went around and around until finally Téa could grind the tough beans on her own. "Good job." Mother rewarded her with a tender rubbing on her head, removing her hand as soon as she remembered the wounds were not completely healed.

"Lola, warm fresh milk for the migote." Lola obeyed.

"Sorry mother, but there's only enough for one." Lola grabbed the empty tub and was about to head out to the cowshed when mother stopped her. "Do it later. Just use the condensed milk for now." Téa couldn't believe her ears. She didn't move. *Deny, deny, and deny*, that was her plan, or so she thought.

"Wow, the condensed milk feels kind of light. Mother didn't we open this can a few days ago?" Lola said while she gave the near empty can to her mother.

"Téa?" Mother exclaimed as she held and shook the can effortlessly in midair. Téa shrugged her shoulders as if she were surprised and had no knowledge of whom had polished off most of the sweet milk, "What?" Téa tried her best to sound innocent.

Nano looked at Téa and shook her sleeve to get her attention, "Téa, did you drink it all?" Nano sang naively.

Mother appeared as if she were trying not to laugh. "Well...? Téa did you?" Téa, stumped for answers, said nothing, but held her head down and nervously shuffled her feet as she listened to her sister giving a lecture.

"Food, you eat food when you are hungry!" shouted her sister. "You don't empty a whole can of store bought sweet milk!" Lola was upset.

"I'm sorry, I wasn't going to, but somehow...I did." Téa forgot to deny her involvement as she helplessly told on herself.

Mother finally cracked a smile. "Lola...enough," she said handing her the empty tub.

"You're never going to learn a thing are you?" Lola mumbled between her teeth as she passed by her sister.

Téa looked pitiful as she wondered about her punishment. "Please don't tell Papa," she said, hoping her mother would have mercy.

Mother turned around as she heard the water boiling. She removed the pot just in time before it began to splash all over the stove.

"Téa, I honestly don't know what I'm going to do with you," she said as she scooped a few spoonfuls of coffee into the boiling water. "I'm running out of options, and ideas to punish you as well." Téa felt no threat in her mother's voice, but her ease didn't last long. "I must think of something before your father does."

Lola came back with the pitcher full of fresh warm milk and soon breakfast was on the table. Lola gave Téa a sympathetic look and said, "Mother, I need help with the milk delivery." Lola was trying to save her sister from a big *sopapo* which is the local Spanish way of saying *ass whipping*.

"I think I just found you a helper," Mother said as her head turned towards the offender.

The next day Téa's sister tried to wake her up too early for her taste, "Leave me alone! It's not morning yet!" Leaving her warm spot next to her brother seemed too painful, but her sister was going to pull down the covers as many times as necessary to get Téa up to work. When that didn't work, the exasperated Lola threatened to drench Téa with cold water. Nano ended up pushing her out of the bed with his little feet. Téa thought of the condensed milk and immediately regretted what she had done. Huffing and puffing she dragged herself to the bathroom.

Breakfast was already on the table and their mother had just finished wrapping a few bocadillos for the day. Téa wondered what the sandwiches were made of, but knowing her mother, she was sure they would be delicious. But Téa was still worried about one thing, she did not want to leave the house with her head looking the way it did.

"Mother, I can't leave the house with my head looking like this," Téa cried, hoping her mother would take pity on her and change her mind, but she didn't. Mother placed her hand in one of the pockets of her apron and pulled out what Téa thought was a handkerchief to dry her teary eyes. To her surprise, it was a headscarf. Mother didn't hesitate to wrap it around her daughter's head. "Here Téa, no one will notice, and if anyone asks why you are wearing a scarf, you tell them...to mind their own business."

Lola gave her sister a reassuring compliment and rushed to grab the bag with the bocadillos while pulling Téa's shirt with a rushing tug. Two of Téa's older brothers had the small donkey saddled with two large metal jugs of fresh milk. Even though there was no need, Father was outside holding the donkey, Rosalia, by its rein. The noble animal had been walking the same daily route for so many years that it was all the donkey knew. It probably could have made the entire trip on its own.

Téa named the animal Rosalia after a girl at school that reminded her of an ass, but that was before she got to know her donkey. She got the giggles every time she said the girl's name out loud, but now feels bad for the donkey. Téa realized way too late that the hard working animal didn't deserve to be named after such a despicable girl.

The next few mornings were spent following her sister around learning the trade of a good merchant. In no time Lola had Téa doing her job. Téa knew Lola was impressed, because she would pat her back and smile at her every time they walked away from a delivery. At home their mother would count the money and say the same thing every evening, "Another hard day has been rewarded by the Lord, let's be thankful for the fruit of our daily efforts."

Téa's first communion was drawing closer, and her mother decided that the traditional white patent leather shoes would have to be replaced with more affordable shoes made out of cloth. Téa pleaded and begged her mother for the traditional and more sophisticated leather ones; it was important to her to be like the other girls. Mother simply said that it was ridiculous to waste that much money on shoes she would only wear once. Mortified, Téa realized she must find the way to make extra money to buy the shoes she wanted.

Lola had her boyfriend meet them every morning, making Téa's life a living hell. The dominant sister had persuaded Téa to go on by herself while she spent her time sitting with her beloved under a tree holding hands and little else. Lola left her younger sister unsupervised and in charge of the milk distribution.

Thankfully, Téa was a fast learner. One day after taking payment from one of the customers, she overheard a conversation in which a woman was talking about how her little girl didn't like the heavy taste of whole milk and that just adding a little water took care of the problem. The girl now drank the entire glass of milk without giving her a hard time.

Téa thought about it and smiled. Her eyes grew wider as she realized that her brilliant idea would grow her funds and provide her with her dream shoes.

For once Téa was happy and relieved that Lola's idiot boyfriend was around to entertain her authoritarian sister. Because of him, her plan had a chance.

The astute girl carefully counted the cups of milk delivered and added just enough water to give her a few extra coins without raising suspicions. She hoped to soon have enough money to purchase a new pair of shiny white patent leather shoes.

All was going well, until one afternoon a customer paid Téa's mother a visit to complain about the low quality of the milk. Mrs. León couldn't believe someone would question the quality of her milk. The thought of anyone suggesting that her family would tamper with the milk made her ill. Yet, knowing of her younger daughter's affinity for trouble, she knew it had to be her.

Téa couldn't believe her luck. Soon after the lady left, she received the biggest sopapo in the history of sopapos. Téa's mother made her go door to door and return the milk money and give the victims their well-deserved apology; along with a complimentary bottle of fresh milk, whole and pure this time.

"Mother, why give them money and milk? Wasn't the apology and the milk enough? It was definitely cheaper to buy me the shoes," Téa complained without realizing how insolent she sounded. Her mother couldn't believe her ears and slapped her over the head in outrage. This time she didn't apologize for hurting her.

The scorned girl made it to her first communion with a burning ass, and her head barely in one piece wearing a veil that hardly stayed on the four hairs she had left on her head. On her feet she wore the most hideous pair of cloth shoes ever made. After the milk incident, there hadn't been money for new ones, even if they were made of cloth. Téa had to wear her everyday shoes.

Of course the shoes didn't go unnoticed by the mean girls. Téa wanted to punch their faces, but she hadn't had breakfast yet. The communion homily took forever, and Téa was more tired than upset. The children had to stand for a very long time and while Téa was very hungry, she still took joy in knowing that every single girl who had made fun of her was rubbing their ankles in pain as their new shiny patent leather shoes did the torturing for her.

After the priest's long monologue, the holy man announced it was time. Téa was fortunate to be first in line. The virtuous priest awaited with his perpetual smile. Téa opened her mouth as soon as she made it to the altar, and the holy man recited something in Latin with his eyes closed before placing the virginal circular cookie over her tongue. With the same right hand, he drew with his fat thumb the sign of the cross on Téa's forehead while mumbling his blessing in Latin. Téa made the sign of the cross on her chest and promised herself to never come back. She found church boring.

No one was allowed to sit until every boy and girl had taken Holy Communion. She preferred being on her knees. At least kneeling was better than standing, especially with her butt still hurting. With her feet saved from blistering and more comfortable than a pig in mud, she enjoyed her Holy cookie. Instead of chewing it, as the priest had ordered, she slowly let the body of Christ melt in her mouth.

Téa pretended to pray, while once in a while opening one eye wide enough to take a good look at the two perfectly symmetrical lines of suffering girls, who like marching penguins dressed in white, made their way painfully slow to the altar and back. By the grace of God her hunger had gone and she was in heaven.

CHAPTER THREE

# *Birds*

"Hush Nano, you don't want to scare them away just yet," she whispered to her little brother. They were hiding in silence in an open meadow waiting for small birds to fly over, hoping they would land beside the large net Téa had camouflaged among the grass so perfectly. "They're too far from our trap yet."

Téa had scattered a handful of bird seed along the side of the net. All she needed was for one bird to spot the food and begin its nervous dance picking on the grain; that was usually sufficient to alert the rest of the flock to his find. Eventually, the entire flock would gather foolishly in just the right spot, and all Téa had to do was pull the string, releasing the large net and hopefully catching most of them.

The day was perfect. The sun was bright, and the breeze stirred the scent of wild flowers as it softly caressed her short hair. She stayed low, watching the trap like a feline; head buried in the long dry grass. Bees buzzed around her, but Téa didn't move at the constant threat. She knew to remain calm, and eventually they would fly away. After all, spring was in full bloom and they were everywhere collecting the sweet nectar. She had always admired bees, such hard working little insects dedicating their entire life to serving their Queen. Téa learned much about these little creatures when Father took her and Nano to a nearby farm where the owner raised them. She was blown away to learn just how much honey one single hive could produce. The farmer would extract the yellow amber using a large spinning machine that pulled the honey from the wooden frames where the bees had built their waxy honeycombs.

Distracted and thinking about sweet honey, she almost missed her opportunity. The birds were all in position, and Téa's hand was ready to pull. Suddenly, her little brother started to clap very loudly. "Nano! You idiot!" Téa pulled the string anyway, but her net was no match for the fast flying creatures.

"I love them," Nano whimpered. Téa couldn't say anything harsh and gave him a tender nudge on top of his head.

"I love them too Nano, you know that right?" Nano nodded. "But Father loves them too."

"Father loves to eat them!" he cried.

"I know. I wouldn't call it love, but anyways, help me with the net would you?" Téa said as she tried to open the net again.

"I don't want to," Nano whined.

"Fine, go home." She pushed him softly. Nano bounced back and hugged her.

"I'll be home soon," she yelled as he ran down the narrow sand path towards their house. Téa kept her eyes on him until her brother was just a small dot in the distance.

She missed him already. Her heart felt heavy as she once again focused on catching the little rascals. Going back empty handed would definitely infuriate her father. The thought of Father giving her a taste of his anger not too long ago still haunted her. Téa's head was still recuperating from the wounds.

She decided to leave the net in its original spot, hoping the birds wouldn't come back. She lay on her back and marveled at her view of the blue sky. It was like a movie screen where the white clouds made all kinds of different shapes. She first saw a bunny, a bird and a choo-choo train. Téa's breathing became deep;

her eyelids began to feel very heavy, and a cozy tingling was caressing her head, helplessly luring her to sleep. She could no longer resist, and she drifted asleep just long enough to be visited by a dream. She dreamed that thousands of bees were making their home on her face. Téa awoke to her brother Antonio laughing hysterically at the sight of his sister slapping her face every time he tickled her with a dry weed.

She had never liked being awoken, and her mood showed it. She wiped the drool from her face and cursed at her older brother. Still drowsy, Téa stood up, but immediately fell back on the soft bed of grass making her more aggravated than before.

"Nice! Now what? These birds will never get close enough for me to catch them. Because of you, I'm going to get in trouble."

"Really? And what do you call *that* little sister?" Antonio pointed to the net. A decent flock had been caught and were frantically struggling to fly away.

"Well, I could have done that without your help," Téa said.

"Really? How? Maybe your snores magically bored them to the net?" Her brother laughed.

"I was not asleep; I was resting my eyes! I have a cold, that's why I snore," she said, embarrassed. "Please don't tell father."

"I won't," Antonio said. "Go home, I'll finish this."

Later that evening, her brother Antonio arrived with Father. She couldn't help but to worry that her father would be mad, and she hoped with all her heart that her brother kept his promise.

Mother would grab the little chirpers one by one from the net as they desperately fluttered and tried to escape the human hand. With a subtle twist, she broke their little necks until the room eventually became silent. With all of them in her lap, she stripped the little birds of their feathers until clean. With Téa looking, mother threw handfuls of the birdies into the fryer, so casually and cold that Téa forgot how merciful she really was. She fried them until they were crispy. It was too much work, but it was father's favorite dish, and mother wanted to please him.

Thankfully, Nano didn't see the birds. He was out front playing under the two giant white mulberry trees that had been there since before the family moved in. The farmhouse didn't belong to them, but they were allowed to live there rent free as long as the family worked the fields and gave the owners their share. The fruit of their labor was used to feed the family, and sometimes there was a little more. All that in exchange for a house that was falling apart and had no running water.

They all took turns bringing full buckets of water from the well. Even little Nano would try to help. He made more of a splash, but he liked to feel useful. They were so thankful to have a roof over their heads.

The patriarch was a member of the rural police and was in charge of keeping Mrs. Milargos' crops safe from thieves. Armed with a rifle, he donned his wide-brimmed hat and covered kilometers of estate lands on the horse he called his own, but the equine was provided under the same rules of the house. Antonio León and his silver tongue made arrangements with the bank to loan him enough money to buy two cows and a bull. The animals did their job very well, and now the family owned a decent amount of cows and the same bull. Antonio was proud and paid the bank in full, once again borrowing more money to buy chickens, geese and pigs.

Father took pride in his looks. He wore his hat straight and was often confused for Señorito Andaluz, which is what a master or landlord is called in Andalucia. The older brothers worked the fields, and the care of the animals was left to Mother and the oldest sister. Téa and Nano did what they could to help as well.

The feast was ready faster than expected and her mother asked Téa to go fetch her little brother.

She found Nano in his usual spot, under the mulberry trees. She called his name, but he was so engaged with drawing in the sand with a stick that he didn't hear a thing.

To Téa's surprise, her little brother was not drawing. He was actually using the stick to disturb a trail of ants.

"Why don't you leave them alone? You felt sorry for the birds, but look at you now," Téa complained.

"I am not hurting them; I am helping. I'm rescuing them from their kidnapers," Nano said without taking his eyes off of his task.

"What do you mean?" Téa was now curious.

"See? The bigger ants are taking prisoners from this ant trail, and I'm liberating them with my stick," he said proudly. "Here little one, you're free to go," Nano whispered.

Téa was taken by his sensitivity; most boys are quite the trouble makers. "Come on, Mother wants you to get ready for dinner."

"Wait, let me free one more!" His sister had to drag him away, otherwise he would have to free the entire colony of ants.

Inside, the round wooden table was set with plates full of beef and potato stew. In the center sat two big bowls of fried birds that the hungry older brothers were attacking between spoonfuls of stew.

They washed their hands and rushed to the table. Nano sat beside Téa like always. Nano didn't waste time and began to dig into the loaf of bread, dipping it into the stew's gravy. It was still too hot for his soft palate. Nano watched in disbelief at how his big brother didn't flinch at the scalding hot food hitting the inside of his mouth.

Father looked at his youngest son tenderly and handed him a little bird to try. "Here have one."

Nano shook his head with a mouthful of soaked bread.

"Oh! Come on, swallow what is in your mouth and try one. They are very good," Father assured him.

"I don't want to," Nano said shaking his head.

"Come on, open your mouth and have one," he asked calmly.

"No," he said again as he looked with terror at the food that didn't look like a bird anymore.

"Open your mouth." Father ordered. Nano didn't. "Open your mouth." Father's happy demeanor had disappeared. "Open your mouth," he commanded. "Boy, open your mouth or else!" Father slapped the frightened boy's head.

Nano cried, still refusing the bird, but his father was determined to make him eat it. Father grabbed Nano's little head and pushed the crusty little bird into the boy's closed mouth. Somehow Father's hand forced Nano's mouth open, even though it had been sealed shut. With no mercy, he forced his child to chew the bird by placing one hand on top of his little head and the other under his jaw.

Téa had never seen her mother look at her father with such hatred. Unable to take any more, mother got up and took her son from him. "That's enough! You...you are a monster!" My father knew he had crossed the line for his wife to interfere.

Nano, sweating with fear, cried and cried as his mother rocked him on her lap until he eventually calmed down and fell asleep in her arms. She tucked him into bed. Téa couldn't help but join him and stroke his soft hair as he sucked on his thumb. Téa eventually fell asleep, waking up to darkness and chills. Nano never wet their bed, but father had scared him so badly that they both woke soaked in his urine. Unfortunately, the bed wetting incident didn't stop there. He began to wet the bed nearly every night. Téa was constantly waking up with damp chills, but was always too sleepy to change the bed sheets, so she just went back to sleep. She had nightmare after nightmare that one minute she was in a flood, and the next in the Arctic. Fortunately her mother thought of a remedy, diapers. They had to be custom made as Nano wasn't a baby anymore. Thanks to their mother's ingenuity, Téa and Nano slept dry again. Mother never complained, not once.

## CHAPTER FOUR

# The Secret

Just being a woman in the 1950's was hard, then add the difficulty of running a farm to the picture.

Mrs. León was a good mother and an even better wife. Her husband was often gone the entire day and sometimes even patrolling the fields at night. This left her with no choice but to deal with situations that were typically dealt with by men. Fortunately, she was tougher than most men so this wasn't a problem. Mrs. León was always busy and had little time for details or extravagances. When she cooked, she cooked in bulk. This was to be expected in a family of ten where everything was done in bulk.

It was her oldest daughter's birthday, Lola was turning seventeen. Mother would bake a carrot cake to honor her day using the same old recipe that had been passed down from generation to generation. She would bake this cake for any special occasion. Gifts were never exchanged in the León house; just the simple cake shared over a cup of coffee or milk. An oversized candle was rescued from one of the kitchen's drawers each time there was a birthday party. As the years passed, the celebrations seemed to occur less and less. The boys were older now and considered these little gatherings childish. Father and Mother never seemed to have time to celebrate their own birthday. The family carrot cake tradition now seemed to be left to Nano, Téa and at least for this year, Lola.

  Carrot cake was a mystery to Téa. Téa hated carrots, but add them to cake batter, mix in some sugar, and that changed everything. The only way she would be caught eating those nasty roots was in a cake. Téa especially loved how her mother gave the cake its finishing touch; a shower of pine nuts so heavy you couldn't see the actual cake.

  Thankfully there were plenty of pine trees on a nearby hill, and collecting the tiny seeds was literally a walk in the park. All Téa and Nano had to do was go for a walk, and pick up the fallen mature pine cones with their scales opened exposing the seeds. The two would then sit around a tree stump and, like monkeys, patiently pick out the seeds one by one with their little fingers, emptying each and every cone.

Proudly, Téa and Nano would hand mother a bag full of the seeds and the entire family would gather around the kitchen table to carefully crack the tiny seeds open with a small rock. Téa would always have to fetch more pine seeds because the family would eat more nuts than they saved. Téa didn't mind; she got to eat them too. Truth be told, she enjoyed the stories her father told around the kitchen table more than the work. There were stories about past times, better times. He told them seemingly forgetting any hardships, loveless weddings, deaths and diseases that were apparently taken in good spirits in the old days. Everyone listened attentively, to the point that you could hear a pin drop when father would pause. Téa was always ready for any kind of fun, but stories and food were among her favorites.

Téa's hair had slowly grown a few inches, and she had never been more appreciative. At least now no one could see the gashes on her scalp. It was still too short, and she looked like a boy, but at least it was not as embarrassing to venture out. She still didn't feel confident enough to wander far from the farm. Just the same, Téa was thankful she didn't have to wear that ridiculous headscarf anymore.

As punishment for allowing the milk incident to happen, Mother had taken away Lola's privilege of seeing her beloved boyfriend indefinitely. Poor Lola saw this as the worst punishment she could ever receive; it was pure torture. She was miserable to say the least. Since it was her birthday, her mother relented and sent Téa to Emilio's house to invite him.

At first Téa refused to go that far, but no matter how hard she cried, her mother was unmoved.

When she finally pulled herself together, Téa took her sweet time walking towards the fence that marked the start of the town road while trying to come up with a way to go into town without being seen or recognized. Emilio's house was in town, and that meant she would have a very long walk. She sat on the stoop outside the fence and with her head resting on her arms, tried to come up with something, but her creative juices seemed to have run dry. *God, if only you could make it rain.* Téa never prayed, but she felt like it this time. Not that she didn't believe in God; she just didn't like the church. She decided to be on her way and get her errand over with before she got in trouble again.

As expected, there were people on the streets. Once in town, Téa hid in the entrance hall of each opened door she happened to find. She would wait until the coast was clear, then be on her way. *My God this is going to take forever.* Téa was breathing hard, and the coast wasn't about to get clear any time soon.

Mercifully, and to Téa's surprise, it began to rain. The people on the streets ran for cover as if it were raining acid, and Téa wasted no time getting on her way. When she reached Emilio's house, she was drenched, but no one had seen her. Téa knocked, and the door opened right away. Emilio's mother didn't recognize her at first, but a look of recognition crossed her face when Téa asked to see Emilio. "He's not home," the busy woman said as she welcomed Téa in and sat her by Emilio's grandmother, who seemed to be forgotten, out of the way, and warming her crooked looking carcass by the fire.

There was not a real need for a fire, but Téa knew old people always tend to be cold. She sat by the old woman, and her conscience was at peace. The deed was done, and her safety was secured. It wasn't her fault Emilio wasn't home. For the first time since her encounter with father scissors, Téa was relieved to have short hair. The fire soon had her short locks and clothes dried and was now baking her bones.

She wanted to move away from the fire, but Granny gave her the look each time she moved. Téa didn't want to be rude. The old woman stared at her and smiled from time to time with her mouth opened revealing the absence of teeth. It sort of scared Téa, especially when she pointed her long deformed finger at her. "Boy, aren't you too young to be friends with my grandson?" Téa was surprised; not because the old lady had confused her with a boy, but that she could compose words and make sense with no teeth.

"I'm not a boy."

"You're not?"

"No ma'am, I'm not."

"Oh! Yes you are!" she giggled, making a whistling sound which was really eerie to Téa. The old woman continued whistling as her teary eyes studied Téa. Téa couldn't wait to get out of there.

"Ma'am, I have to go," Téa said to Emilio's mother when she caught her passing by.

Téa left without giving her a chance to walk her out.

The rain had stopped, but only for a minute or two, and the town's people stayed in their houses waiting for it to reappear. This gave Téa the opportunity to return home without being seen by a single person. She was just a few yards from the wooded fence that surrounded Mrs. Milagros' country estate when she spotted Emilio sitting on the rail. He was chewing on the stem of a mustard plant, the small yellow flowers dancing up and down as he dug dirt out of his fingernails.

"Hey pixie!"

"Don't call me that."

"I'm sorry, let me try again...Howdy boy!"

Téa suspected that he hated her as much as she hated him, but knowing the asshole was invited to her sister's birthday, Téa had to go easy on him.

"What are you doing here? Trying to get a glimpse of my sister?" She wanted to say something hurtful instead.

"Now boy, why don't you get lost?" Téa was very close to losing her temper with him.

"I was actually looking for you." Emilio looked at her sideways, not sure what to think.

"It's about my sister...but you're making it difficult.. I'm having second thoughts..."

"Now, Téa, you better not be messing with me?" he said spitting out the yellow flower.

Emilio's voice threatened Téa, but she acted as if she wasn't fazed, "Now, now...there is no need to get upset."

"Look who is talking!" he shouted at her. "You better tell me what's up or else."

"Excuse me?" Téa's voice almost trembled, giving her away, but Emilio didn't notice, "Why should

I? You want to be rewarded for being an asshole?" Téa said as she walked away.

"Oh, come on! I'm sorry!" he hollered. "You little shit," he said quietly between his teeth.

"My mother wants you to come to Lola's birthday!" she yelled as she walked backwards. "Come around six and make sure to look your best," Téa advised him as she left. "Ah, I forgot. Make sure you bathe and wear cologne, my parents love cologne." She smiled all the way home. She knew the dumb ass would overdo it; he was always trying to impress.

Lola was so nervous at the thought of seeing Emilio again that she couldn't sleep, couldn't eat, and was only able to sit. Téa couldn't understand what the fuss was about; it had not been that long.

Lola joined Téa and Nano, and all she could talk about was Emilio. Miserable, Téa wished someone merciful would shoot her. Nano fell asleep out of boredom... lucky him. Téa's thoughts drifted. She was having trouble understanding what her sister saw in that corn head anyway.

The next morning, Mother had the carrot cake in the stone oven making the house smell sweet for a change. The smell made Téa hungrier than ever. Lola stayed busy preparing for Emilio's arrival.

Five-thirty came, the table was ready with the cake in the middle, and the water for the coffee was about to boil. Lola kept checking one of the windows.

Six-thirty came around and Téa couldn't believe the dumb ass was not there yet. She couldn't help the smirk of satisfaction on her face because for once, he was getting in trouble and she was not.

Lola had always had a healthy appetite, but not when she was nervous or under stress.

Just one look from Antonio León to his wife and Téa knew Emilio's time had run out. She began to serve the coffee for the cake. Poor Lola didn't dare to plea for more time. Mother placed the oversized candle in the center of the cake and moved it in front of the birthday girl. Given her daughter's sadness, mother assumed this would be her last birthday party. The family sang 'Happy Birthday', and she blew the candle so softly it didn't blow out. Lola half-heartedly gave it another try. Father knew she was buying time when she hesitated for a second. Nano, who was sitting by her side, blew it out for her. She thanked him sarcastically as everyone laughed and clapped. Lola's face displayed the saddest, most insincere smile ever. Mother stood behind Lola and gave her daughter an affectionate pat on the back. She then moved between her and Nano and cut a huge piece for Father and then another one of equal proportion for the birthday girl. Lola ate her piece in two bites hoping for a quick end to the festivities. Everyone was impressed, everyone but Nano who was more interested in getting someone to light the candle again.

There was a loud knock on the door making Lola jump out of her seat. Mother pushed her down into a chair while father left the table to answer the door. Lola's face had a look of panic.

"There you are boy! I hope you have a good explanation, and it better be that someone died or you are not seeing my daughter again." Antonio León never bluffed. Lola almost hoped that someone died.

"Sir, with all my respect, my grandmother died." As difficult as it was to take Antonio León by surprise, that did it. Needless to say, Lola's father invited him in and with his arm around his shoulder walked him to his daughter's side.

"Here, have a piece of cake," Mother said as she cut a piece. "I'm so sorry for your loss." Emilio was unfazed.

"Thank you Señora. My granny was just too old, actually older than Methuselah I think. I guess it was just her time." Emilio said it so nonchalantly that everyone stopped eating and looked at him with uncertainly.

Lola's face was the only one with a smile.

"Oh boy, you smell nice!" Mother said as she stood behind him. Téa wished Emilio would turn around and catch a glimpse of her mother's face just to erase his arrogant smirk. Mother pinched her nose with one hand and with the other was able to place a serving of cake in front of the visiting skunk. Everyone smelled the cheap cologne as soon as her father opened the door, but no one had the heart to make fun of him in front of Lola. She was lucky it was her birthday.

Téa couldn't take her eyes off her sister. She had seen that look before, that pale look people get right before they vomit. Téa slowly took a step back.

"Happy Birthday dear!" Emilio said as he held her close and gave her a kiss on her cheek. Téa started to count down out loud. Emilio was confused as to why Téa was suddenly counting backwards as she continued to step away. It was perfect timing. As soon as he returned his attention to his fiancé, there it was, a torrent of carrot cake chunks mixed with undigested pine cone seeds and coffee all over the skunk. For Téa, the finale was better than fireworks. Everyone was too busy trying to look away to notice her big smile.

After the vomiting incident things between Emilio and Téa went from bad to worse. Mother allowed the young lovers to see each other, but only under the condition that Téa served as chaperone. Téa had to follow her sister everywhere, every time Emilio came for a visit. "Mother's orders, like a leech". Téa would say smiling.

"Téa, don't you have better things to do than to follow us?" Lola tried.

After realizing it bothered them, "Nope," is all Téa would answer. Just a simple nope every time, infuriating both lovers. Emilio tried to bribe her but nothing worked, Téa was on a mission and nothing pleased her more than seeing her favorite asshole suffer, but eventually Emilio paid her two reales for each hour she left them alone, Téa wished she had thought of this before the milk fiasco, but c'est la vie. Mother didn't want Lola alone with that corn head, but a little bit of corn never hurt anyone, Téa thought as she counted her money.

For the first time Téa seemed to have forgotten about her short hair, thinking instead of all the candy she could buy with her new found money. Nano was bedazzled with his sister's ability to supply candy. They sat under the shade of a tree and licked on suckers. For hours they stared at nothing and not a single word was exchanged. There was only the sound of the wind through the tree branches and the slurps from their sticky mouths.

Fed up with eating candy, they decided to climb a fig tree and play 'Captain of the Ship'. As Téa was giving orders to her First Lieutenant, Nano found a lizard and proudly shoved it so close to his sister's face that she couldn't tell what it was. Without warning, Téa passed out as soon as she realized what it was. The next thing she remembered was waking up with Nano sitting on her chest crying, "I killed my sister!" Poor Nano was inconsolable. Téa was so dizzy from the fall that she couldn't move her body or her mouth, nevertheless she tried, "Nano." She sounded ghostly.

Nano kept crying with his head buried on his sister's chest. "Nanooooo," she mumbled.

"Sis, don't be mad at me," he said between sobs with his face still on her chest.

"I didn't mean to send you to heaven."

Téa couldn't let such an opportunity pass by. "It's okay Nano, I love it here." Téa tried to sound far away.

Nano began to cry with a passion, his tears rolling down his face.

"Nano, don't cry." Téa's ghostly voice sounded convincing. He didn't stop. "Nano stop...or...I'll take you with me to heaven," she said again in her ghostly voice.

Nano had his head buried against Téa, continuing to cry. Finally his crying came to a stop, but not before he lifted his head, took his sister's shirt, and used it to blow his nose. Téa couldn't react in time to stop him.

When he saw Téa coming back from the dead he moved his little red face and smiled. Téa was now in a sitting position when he pushed her back to the ground with a hug. "You're back!"

"Yep, I'm back! Full of snot and all...you did it kiddo," Téa said in her normal voice.

"Did I do that? How Téa? How did I bring you back?"

Not wanting to disappoint him, Téa said the first thing that came to her mind. "Your snot did it," she said. Téa didn't feel bad because in a way, it was true, the snot was responsible for the game to be over.

They walked home with Nano pinching her once in a while, just to make sure his sister was real.

"Hurry up we have to get you home in time for choir practice. We don't want to make Mother mad. By the way, don't tell anyone about your magic snot, let it be our little secret," Téa made sure to tell her little brother. The last thing she needed was another whipping. Nano shook his head several times. Mother met them at the door and immediately took Nano by the hand and headed for the church.

It was Holy week and Mother made him join the church choir. Téa was content to be left alone. She jumped on her bed, and before she could enjoy her solitude for too long they were back. She left her room to find Nano crying on Mother's lap.

"What happened Mother?" Téa asked. "Was he too shy to sing in front of the priest?"

Mother ignored Téa and went straight to their room with Nano in her arms. She placed Nano in his giant diaper and left him there to cry himself to sleep. Téa felt sorry for him so she laid beside him.

As Téa held him Nano grew quiet, "Nano, why were you crying?"

"My snots are not magical anymore." Téa realized what her little game had produced unforeseen events, and she nervously went to see Mother.

Mother was sitting at the table telling her sister Lola what had happened. "We arrived early and a funeral mass was being officiated by Father Rogelio. We sat there in the back waiting for the service to end. Suddenly your brother, who was sitting on my lap, went straight up to the widow who was saying her last goodbyes to her dead husband in his coffin. He just stood there beside her... I thought that was so sweet of him, wanting to console the grieving woman. But then Nano pulled on her sleeve, and to my horror climbed up on the open coffin and began to blow his nose on her dead husband." Téa had never seen her sister laugh so hard. Lola had to excuse herself and go to the bathroom, because she had already peed her pants.

"Why was he doing that?" Lola asked when she finally regained her composure.

"He said it was a secret." Thankfully Téa's mother had no clue, as to Téa's mischief. Téa gave a slight giggle and a sigh of relief, at least for now.

CHAPTER FIVE

# The Kite

To Téa's regret she had to break the bad news to her little brother about the loss of his snot powers. For his sake she tried to do it in a way that would cause him as little distress as possible.

"Nano, you ought to know that nothing in this life lasts forever, and your snot powers didn't either."

"But why?" His chin shook like jelly as his little voice trembled with emotion.

"I don't know...it's just the way it is," Téa said. Nano stared at the floor hugging himself. Téa was about to explode with remorse.

"Dear, I lied... It was just a joke that went too far. Nano, would you forgive me?" He slowly lifted his head and nodded.

"Can I have a hug?" Téa asked. He gave her a sad nod but didn't move. Téa grabbed him and gave him a hug, a very long one. "I'm sorry Nano." Téa was sincere. "I love you brother," she whispered in his ear. "I love you bigger," Nano whispered back.

"I tell you what, I'm going to make you a surprise present!"

"What is it?" Nano had to ask.

"If I tell you, it wouldn't be a surprise anymore!" She grabbed his little hand and made him follow her.

"Where are we going?"

"You'll see!" Téa sang.

She took her little brother to the family who lived on the hill next to them. The Varea family had twin boys that looked nothing alike, one had white blonde hair, fair skin and blue eyes while the other one had brown hair, dark skin and hazel eyes. Their house had no land to work and provide for their family. Téa's mother would often visit bringing a bag with food, eggs, potatoes and a few seasonal vegetables. The generous Mrs. León would sometimes add a chicken as well. Their daily stew usually consisted of a single potato and a few greens. One day she decided to bring two birds instead, a hen and a rooster. "These are not for the stew, you hear? These are meant for making more chicks," Mrs. León advised Mrs. Varea.

The birds didn't waste time and soon the Vareas were surrounded with so many chickens that they didn't know what to do. The León brothers, with Father directing, helped Mr. Varea build a chicken pen. Mrs. Varea was very thankful. Now that they could sell the eggs and chickens, they were doing much better. The León's were happy, and the Vareas couldn't wait to repay their kindness.

With the chicken business booming, the Vareas purchased two pigs; one of the piglets was given to Mrs. León as a small token of appreciation, and the other was theirs. The piglet, who was kept near the house, was growing quickly on a diet of leftovers, but as he continued to grow, so did his appetite. What used to fill him up, was now just an appetizer. Hungry for more, he ate whatever came across his path. The Vareas once had a big problem with rats, but the pig soon took care of it. The pig ate the rats, some as big as rabbits. The Vareas were quite happy with their pig. They were delighted that their rat population was soon regulated, but the pig's appetite continued to increase. The leftovers weren't enough and eventually they had to feed him chickens. The pig looked more and more like a monster and sounded like one too. He would growl like crazy at anyone who came near. The last straw was when the pig tried to eat one of the Varea boys. Thank God the father always carried his rifle on his back and shot the monster before he could harm the boy.

The Varea boys were quite the hillbillies. They found shoes to be uncomfortable and an inconvenience. Their feet had grown massive and the bottoms hardened much like old leather. Téa tried to imitate them, but her feet were much too tender for the foliage surrounding the land.

Sam, short for Samuel, and his brother Santi, short for Santiago, had one skill. They were expert kite makers, and Téa wanted to surprise Nano by having them teach him how to make one.

Téa and Nano walked up the hill toward their house. As they came close to the house she yelled their names, "Sam... Santi!" When they didn't respond, she yelled their names again, as did Nano. Finally she spotted the brothers running towards her with big beaming smiles. Regardless of their family's circumstances, the two always seemed to be happy.

"Hey Téa, what's with you?" Sam and Santi might not look like brothers, but they sounded identical.

"I need a favor from you two."

"Shoot!" they both answered.

"Teach my little brother how to make a kite."

"Make a kite? That's all?" Santi said as he looked at Sam. "I think we can do that, don't you Sam?" Sam just nodded as he typically did.

"Well Nano, first things first; we need to fetch some tree sap to use as glue. We have everything else but the sap," Santi said. "To make a kite you need reed for the frame, old newspapers for the body, pieces of cloth for the tail and lots of string so that it will fly high into the sky. You'll see Nano!"

Soon they were back from collecting enough sap to glue an entire house. Sam brought out all the materials to make the kite from the shack located in the back of the house while Santi began to dissolve the sap in a little bit of water. With Nano helping, Téa couldn't help but smile at the sight of her brother. He was in heaven. In no time, the kite was assembled.

"Can we give it a try?" Nano was excited.

"Hell no, you want the kite to fall apart? It needs to dry at least till tomorrow."

"Okay, but can we take it home with us?" Téa asked.

"Nope. It'll break into pieces just the same. We'll bring it to you tomorrow, ok?"

"I guess," Téa said. She and Nano sighed with disappointment as they left.

The next day Téa and Nano waited for the brothers. "When are they coming?" Nano asked.

"I wish I knew, soon I hope." Just a short time later Santi and Sam could be seen running down the hill flying Nano's kite, whistling loudly to get Téa and Nano's attention. Sam had another kite under his arm.

Nano and Téa ran to meet them almost right away. "Wow, you made one for me too? Is that one for me? I hate to assume..." Téa asked.

"No, it's not for you." Santi teased. "It's for your twin sister!" He chuckled. "Ah! Wait, you don't have a twin sister!" Sam gave his brother an evil look.

"Téa, sometimes I wonder. Of course it's for you...who else would my brother spend his entire afternoon making a kite for?" Santi teased. Sam punched his brother so hard Nano's kite broke loose.

Téa had always had a secret crush on Sam.

"And what was that for? Man that hurts!" Santi yelled as the kite flew away.

"Good! I hope it hurts for a long time, you idiot!" Sam was so embarrassed he left without looking at Téa or saying another word.

"Oh, get over it," Santi yelled again.

"Well, I guess it's just you and me!" Santi said arrogantly.

"Well, I guess it's just you and you because I don't play with assholes." Téa grabbed her brother's hand and left without giving him as little as a goodbye.

"Fine, be that way! Grrrr girls... I could definitely do without them. My father once told me: Women, you can't live with them, yet they're everywhere!" Nonchalantly, he left whistling.

Téa took her kite inside and leaned it against the wall. Nano's kite was a fine one, but Téa's was spectacular. Sam really went out of his way for her.

"Téa, are we going to fly your kite?" Nano said sadly.

"Nano we can't right now; I need to find your kite first."

"Can I come with you?"

"No, Nano. I don't know where that kite landed, and I can't watch you...believe me, you'll be better off here playing with your ants."

"You don't have to, I'm a big boy." Téa looked at his little frame and his adorable round face and as hard as it was to tell him no again, she did.

"I'll be back before you know it. The sooner I leave, the faster I'll return. It won't take me long I promise."

Téa ran toward where she thought the kite had drifted. Her eyes were everywhere, especially on tree tops. A few hours passed by and she still had no idea where that kite was.

Téa ended up in front of Mrs. Milagros' huge house. The landlady actually had a mansion, iron gate and all, surrounded by a six foot wall. Through the iron gaps she could see the fantastic garden. The scent of Jasmine was evident, which was actually why she stopped.

"I'll be darned!" Téa exclaimed. The red kite had landed in one of the trees that shielded the big house. Téa looked for a bell or something that would beckon someone to open the gates but couldn't find anything. She yelled a few times, but again, nothing. She had to go back home empty-handed.

Téa remembered overhearing her father tell Mother about Mrs. Milagros' trip to the capital. Mother was glad that the landlady was away for an entire week. Mrs. León and her daughter were to do the general cleaning while the Lady was away. Spring was just around the corner and the place had to be deep cleaned.

The lady of the house didn't want to deal with all the commotion and only trusted Mrs. León. They didn't know it yet, but Téa was going to help too, at least until she got to the kite.

## CHAPTER SIX

# Mrs. Milagros

Mrs. Milagros was the sole heir to her parent's estate. She was old and unhappy. Married at sixteen to Raul Mendoza, she was now a widow. Their marriage had been arranged by their parents and was never consummated as neither cared to fall in love with the other. Mrs. Milagros' heart had already been taken, and so had his. Hers by the love of her youth, and his by a roommate from the university. When her husband finally died of old age, she cursed the stars, *Lord, haven't I suffered enough?* She would mumble between prayers.

    Mrs. Milagros was now in her eighties and had grown accustomed to having him around. A lifetime of an unfruitful marriage was not completely in vain. The two grew to accept their differences, and a friendship was born. Each pretty much did what they pleased, discreetly of course. Everyone thought very highly of them, and they were an institution on how a marriage should be.  Everyone agreed it was unfortunate the Lord never blessed them with a family.

Her cousin's children, Rosina and Marina came as soon as they heard the news of their great uncle's passing, and with the pretext of caring for their old rich aunt; they made her home theirs. Mrs. Milagros knew exactly what was in their minds, and she played it to her advantage. Their aunt's fortune was what enabled them to endure her crankiness and her impossible demands.  With nothing else to do, Mrs. Milagros secretly enjoyed her power trips. She knew no matter how hard she pushed their buttons, she'd always have them eating out of the palm of her hands. "They'll put up with me and my ways as long as I have grain in my sack," Mrs. Milagros would chuckle as she repeated this to the help.

On the morning Mrs. León and Lola were supposed to be on their way to clean Mrs. Milagros' mansion, Téa was still in her warm bed pretending to be asleep and in no hurry to respond to her sister's calls. "I don't know why she volunteers to help if she really doesn't mean it," Lola said.  Téa was having second thoughts about retrieving the kite. It wasn't that she didn't care anymore, it was just the same story every day. Téa wouldn't get up, not even if the house were on fire, but her loving sister was always there ready to wake her with a bucket full of cold water. Téa always pushed her luck to the end.

She made it up just in time, but only after Lola had sprinkled her with a warning spritz before drenching her. Téa left Nano in bed looking so peaceful with his little head lying on his pillow, covered to the neck with white linens surrounding his face. He looked like an angel.

Mother wanted to leave as soon as possible so they could come back in time to cook dinner. Lola reminded her mother that they were already late, and there was no time for breakfast. "It's not like it's going to make a difference, she'll just be hungry again as soon as we get there. She is always hungry." But Mrs. León refused to let Téa go without and gave her a bocadillo to eat on their way.

Mother knew a thing or two about hunger, so she had learned to express her love with food. She would ask strangers that stopped by the water well for a drink of water if they were hungry. Before anyone could answer no, she'd give them a full plate. "It's not nice to refuse a meal, especially when it's given from the heart. Now, I know you are just too polite," Mother would sing without even looking at her guest.

The long walk to Mrs. Milagros' residence was normally easy for Téa, but with no time for breakfast the same hike with just a small sandwich for later, was tortuous.

When they finally arrived in front of the large wrought iron gate, mother dropped her bags on the ground and looked for her bundle of keys. She was tired and took her time. Téa was so hungry she felt as if she were about to be sick. "Here mother, let me help you." Téa took the keys from her hands and nervously tried each of them in the lock. Mrs. León tried to take the keys back in an attempt to speed up the process, but Téa stubbornly snatched them away, believing she could do it faster.

Lola sat on a large stone and started to eat an apple, Mrs. León pulled her daughter out of the way and opened the gate without the keys. The entire time Téa had thought the gate was locked. All this time wasted, when all she had to do was simply pull on the unlocked gate. She felt dumb.

Lola grabbed Téa's hand and shoved the half eaten apple into it. "Here, eat this dumb ass!" Lola said as she took the keys away from her.

In no time, Téa finished the rest of the apple. As she took her time catching up with the others, she discovered the kite had blown away. Téa shook her head thinking that since the padlock was apparently just for decoration, retrieving the damn kite yesterday would have been easier than taking candy from a baby.

The mansion looked grand from the outside of the fence, but once Téa crossed the gates she felt small and overwhelmed with the lavishness. The grandness of the palace reminded her of a spoiled child. Everything looked as if it had been done on a whim. There were French gardens, and the outside of the magnificent structure was painted horizontally with symmetrical thick lines alternating light yellows with a burgundy ochre that defined the elegant Mudejar style, while the interior of the mansion was a fascinating mix of mostly Italian and Chinese designs. The visual treat felt as if the madness of styles was the result of the inability of a capricious princess to make up her mind.

The front of the castle was actually on the opposite side of the ornate iron gate overlooking the ocean. From this, the highest point of the town, you really felt like a queen. A thick row of old stones surrounded the summit for safety and on the inner side they had been molded and shaped into benches. Téa sat on one of the benches admiring the ingenuity of the stones overlapping each other. Between the benches, stones had been carved out, allowing a bed for strange looking plants to grow. The young girl had never seen any of these plants before. One in particular caught her attention. It was the strangest looking of them all. It looked as if a green butter bean had been split open and grown teeth. A quick little ant was crawling on its stem and entered the bean. The ant was quick, but the green toothed bean was quicker. In front of her eyes the bean snapped its conical teeth closed and the little ant was trapped inside. Téa watched with terror at the macabre scene, hoping her brother Nano never had to visit Mrs. Milagros' place and bear witness to this.

Mrs. León called out to Téa, "Don't sit underneath that tree! Can't you see it's full of worm nests?" Poor Téa almost passed out as she looked up and saw the nasty little things wiggling over her head. They were weaved into a see-through sack. Téa felt disgusted, but she couldn't move; neither was she able to take her eyes off their yellow and black stripes as they pushed each other around. The only thing she could reply was, "What?"

"I said...move! Before they fall on your head and pee on you!"

"Why? Pee on me? So what?" Téa whined as her mother pulled her out from under the infested pine tree.

"If that bag full of worms breaks on you, your hair will fall out to never grow back." Téa trembled at the thought of what she might look with bald spots in addition to her already ugly haircut. "I need to remember to tell your brothers to come and take care of this tree before it infests the rest." Mother said.

Téa's brothers were very good at getting rid of pests. Every year wasps would make their nest in the cove where the roof meets the wall. Every year they were removed, and every year they would rebuild their nest back in the same place. Téa looked forward to this event at the end of each summer. The cousins, Nano and the women would gather inside the house and watch from the safety of the screened in window. They would giggle nervously and pinch one another with anticipation as they waited for the show to start.

The brothers came out in the late afternoon, when the wasps were in for the night. They covered themselves from head to toe with heavy clothing, gloves and a hat that surrounded their head with a net, which was necessary as well. Looking as if they were from outer space, they would walk slowly, carrying a long tiki torch that emanated a thick white smoke and place it outside each nest. This was done in order to calm the wasps, or at least make them dizzy. Meanwhile, the other brothers sprayed the nest with poison. The cans were wrapped onto long poles that were fabricated specifically for this task. It was amazing how the men from outer space fought against the malevolent miniature creatures attacking as if they were flying saucers. The entire hive fought back, defending their queen to the death. In the end only a few remained alive, lying on the ground, gasping for air, unable to fly. The nests were then scraped down, as the family came out of hiding, and victoriously took turns stepping on the few remaining wasps.

## CHAPTER SEVEN

# *Salt*

There were many things Téa loved; one of them being the ocean. It was probably right up there with food.

The beach was very close to the León's house. All you had to do was cross the asphalt road and after a brief walk you were there. Téa's mother always warned her children never to go to the ocean by themselves. The beach was on a river delta. At first glance, one would never think the flat surface water, with its peaceful appearance, was dangerous. One might wade in only to find that beneath all that innocence, a hidden whirlpool of strong currents existed that was powerful enough to take down even the most experienced of swimmers. Over the years the hidden currents caused many children and a few adults to drown. Téa couldn't understand what all the fuss was about. She had been swimming there many times and never felt a thing. She was sure Mother was just overreacting.

Since the winds were stronger at the delta, Téa used the kites as the perfect excuse to visit the beach. Using this as an excuse, Téa and Nano went often, but not before mother gave them a lecture about what would happen if she were to find out that they had been swimming. At first, the two just flew their kites. But it wasn't long before Téa began to consider a refreshing swim. Nano questioned her, but it didn't matter. She was convinced they would not get caught. At first they were satisfied just wetting their feet, but when that didn't amuse them anymore, they went a little deeper, just until it reached their knees. It didn't take long, however until the two were swimming in their undergarments. Their time on the beach was perfect; wind and all.

Every day the duo said goodbye and with kites under their arms, quickly walked to the beach. Mother watched from the front porch until they crossed the asphalt road and disappeared into the trail. Their fast pace slowed as they passed the vast patches of bushes and shrubs along the trail packed with surprises; blackberries, wild grape vines and the occasional banana spider, Téa loved to call it a *tarantula* just to get a reaction out of her little brother. She remembered when father brought one home in a glass jar. Nano had stared at the arachnid creature with his nose glued to the glass for hours; jerking back every time the spider moved a leg.

At the end of the path, and before entering the beach, was a paradise called "Las Piletas." The Basins were the entrance-exit to the beach. It was guarded by a giant iron gate that was painted bright Andalusian green, and always wide open. A path of wet red sand guided you to the basins. Leopoldo, the owner, sold *altramuces* and served hundreds of ready-filled glasses of refreshing water. Covering the path were rows of grapevines that over the decades had grown so large that they met the opposite vines and created a cave-like structure. This provided pedestrians with comfortable shade. Also along the trail were benches painted with the same bright Andalusian green. Sometimes Téa and Nano would just sit and watch the other beachgoers walk by.

Once at the beach, Téa and her brother would slip off their clothes and place them on top of the kites. Their shoes topped off the stack, keeping their things from blowing away. That day the wind was stronger than usual, making the golden sand prick their ankles. They sought refuge in the water, while constantly watching their clothes, which were rapidly being covered by the raging sand.

They laughed and splashed and chased one another through the shallow waves until exhaustion struck. Breathing hard, Téa sat on the shore while her brother attacked the waves with a stick. She watched her brother and began to dig in the sand with her hands. Holding her hands in midair, she let the wet sand trickle through her fingers onto her knees. With each handful of sand dropped on her legs, they started to look like futuristic mountains. The sand domes fell every time they grew too high. Nano, now tired, wanted to do the same and sat by his sister.

Digging deeper in the sand, Téa found a few cockles and her mouth salivated. The more she dug; the more she found. *Ah too bad*, Téa thought. Taking the mollusks home would be as good as confessing their sin to their mother. *I could sell them*. Téa smiled, her merchant mind was always at work. Nano's screams dragged her from her fantasy world. She was relieved to see him dancing over the clothes instead of drowning. Téa washed off the sand and quickly went to her brother.

"Our clothes are gone!" Nano cried.

Téa cursed like a sailor and kicked the sand trying to find their clothes. "Damn thieves have taken everything, even our shoes!" Téa kept on kicking.

She began to cry hysterically at the thought of the painful beating she was sure to receive.

"Téa, there's no need to keep looking! Our clothes are gone! Let's go home sister, please!" Nano said.

They looked at each other for a moment and started to run.

The pain the small pebbles inflicted under their feet did nothing to slow them down. It wasn't until they drew close to the end of the trail that they slowed down and hid behind a bush. Téa's heart pounded so hard she felt like vomiting. Nano held his sister's hand, and they both waited for the perfect moment to cross the asphalted road. When the time came, they ran faster than they ever had before. When they finally reached their house, they leaned against the wall of the house and listened carefully for their mother, their sister or anyone at all. The house remained silent. *Could it be that no one is home? If that isn't luck, I don't know what is.* Téa thought.

Fortunately, it was summer, and they changed clothes often, so that wasn't going to be a problem.

Their shoes were a different story; the thieves stole their only pair.

    Before long, Mrs. León and Lola returned home to find that Téa and Nano had already taken their bath. At least that's what Téa told her surprised mother as she and her brother lay in bed for the night. "Oh my, going to bed so early, it's not even dark yet!" Mother was suspicious, but she let it go.

    The next morning Téa was wide awake for a change, thanks to her early bedtime. She could hear Mother wishing Téa's father good night. He was going to bed after working all night keeping Mrs. Milagros' fields safe from thieves.

    Lola had already left to make her milk deliveries, and the house was quiet; at least until Mother's voice began to call Téa.

    Lola had left two glass bottles of milk behind. "Mother, what?" Téa acted sleepy.

    "Good, I'm glad you're up! I need you to deliver these two milk bottles to the Montero's residence." *Great*, Téa thought. *My least favorite family. Too uppity if you ask me, so much so that their help even puts on airs.*

    Téa did what mother asked without complaining, at least not to her face. Two liters of fresh milk delivered daily.

*What are they, cubs? Rich people, they have too much. I wish I was rich.* Téa was annoyed.

"Téa, where are your shoes?" Téa froze.

"I don't know..." Téa said.

"You don't know? Téa don't you leave the house without them," Mother insisted. "You'll hurt your feet!"

"I'll be ok Mother, the Varea brothers don't ever wear shoes, and they are fine," she said as she nervously walked faster.

"Bad influence, those Varea brothers...bad, bad influence that's what they are," Téa's mother said to herself as her daughter hurried out of the front door.

Téa left with the promise of a good breakfast when she got back. Not wanting to explain her lost shoes, she left the house without breakfast and without going to the bathroom, which was normally the first thing she did as soon as she got up.

Trying to take her mind away from her needs, Téa spent the trip to the Montero's house daydreaming. Suddenly, the yummy smell of frying fish hit her. Téa was always ready to eat, and no matter how hard she tried not to think about food; it was impossible.

Thankfully the smoke carrying the delicious smell came from the house where she was to deliver the milk. *Lucky me!* Téa thought. *I am not leaving without a taste.*

She was about to enter the foyer, but stopped because she thought the floor was wet. It wasn't; it was just that clean. Someone had obviously taken their sweet time polishing that marble. Téa knocked on the front door, and a young woman about Lola's age opened it. She was pretty, but her face went ugly as soon as she spotted Téa. Her expression went sour, as if she had eaten a lemon.

"What are you smiling at?" the maid asked.

"Why do you care? I always smile." Téa said the first thing that came to her mind.

"Hasn't your mother taught you any manners?" Téa wanted to punch her, but she couldn't take her eyes off of the maid's white apron. It was so clean.

"Here." Téa was going to carry in the milk, but the maid stopped her cold.

"I'll take it from here... thank you." The maid tried her best to take the bottles from Téa's arms without touching her.

"I need to use the bathroom," Téa said, but again the maid stopped her, this time with the door.

"Not so fast! The servants aren't allowed to use the inside bathrooms. Take the back door and use the kitchen's half bathroom," she said.

"I'm not a..." Poor Téa couldn't finish her sentence, as the snobbish maid had already swung the door shut.

Scorned, Téa turned around and with her legs twisted, tried to walk away. She noticed that the flowerpots placed elegantly along the white walls were reflecting their image vividly on the shiny marble floors. She needed to pee badly, so she did. Téa watered the plants and decided to pee on the floor too, in payback for the maid's nice gesture. No one could tell the difference if it hadn't been for the urine smell.

Satisfied with her deed, she went to the back with the pretext of using the bathroom and the intent of scoring some fish.

The back of the house looked just as neat as the front with its perfectly manicured bushes, and pink and red geranium hanging pots each lined up perfectly. A small door was open allowing the succulent smoke to escape the kitchen. Colorful beaded shutters hung on the upper part of the door making a curtain to keep flies away.

Téa said hello loudly then said it again as the fat shadow of a robust woman moved back and forth immersed in her cooking. She was mumbling a song out of tune. The woman could not sing. The cook screamed when she turned around and saw Téa standing in her kitchen. "Lord have mercy child! You scared me! How long have you been standing there!?"

"Not for too long. I thought you saw me, but I guess you didn't."

"Well yes, I'm very busy, and no, I didn't see you." The robust woman spoke anxiously as she rinsed a deep pot under fresh water.

"I'm so sorry Señora, I tried to get your attention many times but nothing."

"Alright!" She shook her head rushing throughout the kitchen. "What do you want? I don't have all day."

"Oh, yes! I was wondering if I could use your bathroom." Staring at the crispy pieces of fried fish, Téa almost forgot why she was there.

She gave Téa a suspicious look that made her a little nervous. Téa felt as if she could see through her. "Sure, make it quick. I don't have all day." Téa nodded with a smile.

"Did you wash your hands?" The cook asked.

"No, but I'll wash them if you give me a piece of fried fish."

"Oh Lord no, that I can't give you, but it's important to wash your hands after using the toilet. I ask out of habit," she said.

She shook her head again and pointed to the faucet with her eyes strangely empty of lashes.

Téa took her sweet time washing her hands, thinking of a way to sneak a piece unnoticed. "Mmm that fish sure smells good."

She ignored her. "I can't give you any," she said.

"Oh, but why not? It's not like there won't be enough for everyone. Nobody's going to know if an insignificant little piece broke off and went missing. I'm not telling, and you're not telling, so what's the harm?" Téa whined.

"The lady of the house counts everything in the pantry, and when I say everything; I mean everything."

"She counts every piece of fish? You've got to be kidding!" Téa couldn't understand greediness.

"We can only have their leftovers, but by then the fish is cold... not that there are ever any leftovers anyway."

"I don't care if the fish is cold; I'll wait."

"I don't think so. I can't believe you'd invited yourself; you are shameless," the cook said as she fried more fish.

Téa didn't want to steal the fish, but her stomach took over and she had no choice. She positioned herself as close to the table as possible, and as fast as she could grabbed a piece of fish from the top of the pile with the idea of running with it. But, when she grabbed it, the fish was so hot that it burned her fingers and she quickly had to let go. Téa couldn't help but to cry out as the fish rolled off the top of the pile and over it went to the floor. The cook turned around, cursed, and dropped what she was doing to chase Téa around the large table.

"You little piece of shit! I knew you were up to no good!" The cook was furious.

Téa didn't want to laugh, but she was too nervous. The troubled girl was able to rescue the piece of fish from the floor and took off in the direction of the small door, but trying to escape that way was out of the question. The giant woman's body blocked the tiny doorway. Téa had to run in the other direction and cut through the house. Surprisingly, she didn't get lost, but she wasn't out yet. The angry cook and now the rest of the snobby help were running after her. Téa placed the prize in her pocket, because she needed her two hands to open the big door. Téa ran as fast as she could, remembering just in time to avoid the present she'd left behind earlier in the foyer. Like a professional skater, she slid all the way to the end where she was free and clear. The others weren't so lucky.

## CHAPTER EIGHT

# Cactus Flower

Téa was very good at convincing her mother that she loved to go barefoot. She had to be since her only good pair had been stolen. It was almost the end of summer and since the haircut in the spring, Téa had become sort of a tomboy. To get out of her mother's way, she began to visit the gardens outside of Mrs. Milagros' place.

With Mrs. Milagros away, Téa was free to roam the premises lost in her games. She was helplessly drawn back to the strange looking plants that ate bugs; carnivores. Téa would curiously force them open to see how whatever they had caught looked inside of their tummy. She thought it weird to have the stomach and the mouth in the same place.

"I assure you that whatever you are looking for is not in there, especially something this big," a voice assaulted Téa from behind. It was Mrs. Milagros.

"I am so sorry señora," Téa stuttered as she turned around. Expecting a reprimand, nothing could have prepared her for the colorful surprise that awaited in Mrs. Milagros' hands. It was the kite.

"I found this kite tangled in one of my trees. Here, you can keep it. It looks like it was made for a girl, and you are a girl, so here."

Téa was so nervous to be in front of such an important lady, that she didn't know how to react or what to say.

"I don't know what to say," Téa said as the lady walked away.

"Well, a simple thank you should do." She stopped, but didn't turn around. Téa forced a stuttered thank you. "You are León's daughter, right?" Mrs. Milagros asked, knowing full well who she was. "I have heard about you, Téa." Poor Téa didn't know what to think. "Pay me a visit every once in a while, would you?" Mrs. Milagros smiled, but Téa didn't notice. Scared, Téa nodded about a thousand times and said yes, this time without stuttering.

"And Téa?" Mrs. Milagros looked at her this time. "You can stay and play all you want, but leave my plants alone." Téa's eyes grew with fear and her stomach burned. She couldn't move but nodded again.

Satisfied, the lady walked away slowly inspecting her plants as she walked. Stopping by a jasmine bush, she collected some and pressed them against her nose, deeply sighing as her eyes followed Téa leaving. The old lady waved when the girl looked back. Téa didn't.

*Why would a lady of such a rank want anything to do with a country girl like me? Rich people, go figure,* Téa thought as she left.

Téa spent that entire day thinking about Mrs. Milagros and her unusual request. She purposely forgot to mention anything to her mother, hoping the landlady was just being nice.

A few days passed and just when Téa had forgotten about Mrs. Milagros, her mother mentioned the lady's request.

"Téa, I don't know why, but Mrs. Milagros wants you to pay her a visit. Téa are you listening?" Téa had heard her the first time, but she was hoping her mother would leave her alone.

"Yes, I heard you Mother." Téa said.

"Well? When is it going to be?" Mother asked.

"Not today, that's for sure."

"What did you say young lady?" Téa's mother always seemed hard of hearing when she didn't like her daughter's tone.

"Mother, I promise to visit her tomorrow." Téa's answer had a soft polite ring to it. Mother said nothing, just gave her a quick nod.

Today Téa had other plans; she wanted to see Sam. The kite was just the excuse. "Mother, I'm going to the Varea's."

"Why? You have no business running around with those wild boys." Téa's mother had become concerned after her daughter decided she no longer needed shoes. She thought the boys might be a bad influence on her. The last thing Téa needed was help finding trouble.

"Mother! I'm just returning this kite, that's all."

The thought of seeing Sam made her face turn red, and the closer she came to the Varea's house, the hotter her face felt.

Téa could see the small stucco house from afar, but to her surprise no one came to greet her. Not even their dog.

Téa yelled the boys' names, but nothing. Something was wrong, the dog's bowl was upside down, and the wind was slapping the entrance door. Téa's first reaction was to grab a few stones just in case she needed to defend herself.

*I better go*, she thought as her skin flared with goosebumps.

She began to walk backwards, spun around and ran away as fast as she could. Running down the hill her thoughts ran as well. Her imagination was spinning in all directions, and her eyes were wide with fear. Before she knew it, she was going faster than she could manage. A hole in disguise made her lose her balance and fall. She was rolling down the hill, kite and all. Téa screamed as she rolled down the hill, only to be stopped by a magnificently healthy Prickly Pear Cream Cactus growing on the edge of a cliff overlooking an enormously deep drop. These plants demanded respect and were often used as natural fences to keep livestock from wondering off. This one was large and armed with a full body of white, long, bone like thorns that had impaled her face and the rest of her body. Silence.

Téa's face was not bleeding and thankfully her eyes were spared from the piercing. Her body was bruised and covered with dust, sweat and tears. The poor soul was in shock. The slightest movement caused agonizing pain. She tried to scream, but that took too much effort. Téa couldn't move or talk, much less scream. All she could do was lie there and whimper for her mother. She tried, but all she could manage was "ma..."

"Maaaaa!" Téa repeatedly sobbed the only word the thorns allowed her to articulate while the pain made itself present every time she moved.

She prayed for someone to find her, but her hopes faded as the sun dissipated over the horizon. The crickets shyly began their rehearsal of their monotone lullaby, and the scent of honeysuckle was becoming more and more evident. Téa hoped to hear her family yelling her name. She even wished she might be found by the bad guys she supposedly was running from, anything was better than being crucified by hundreds of thorns and attacked by the animal kingdom.

Exhausted, cold and feverish, Téa moved in and out of consciousness, drifting off to a peaceful trance then waking up to her impaled nightmare. In the dark and alone in silence on the countryside hill, the shivering girl was determined to save her strength just in case she needed to alert anyone of her position. A bumblebee roamed around her head. Poor Téa didn't like insects, especially if they could fly. Defenseless with fear, her eyes followed the fat inoffensive bee while the ants helped themselves to her body. She thought of Nano and his determination to save those mean little creatures.

In between sobs, she heard voices. It was her brothers. She mumbled as loud as she could, but her voice was no match for the cactus thorns.

"Antonio, go check the Varea's! They might know where she is!" Mother screamed at Téa's father who was already on his horse galloping towards the Varea's hill. It was dark, and he almost passed his daughter's impaled body unnoticed. If it hadn't been for that one horrific scream Téa had been saving, she would most definitely not have been found that night.

Antonio León couldn't believe his eyes as he stared at his beloved daughter impaled by God only knows how many thorns. His first thought was of how to rescue her without hurting her damaged little body. Antonio León, normally a hard, cold man, had never felt that sort of terror in his heart. In no time he was on the ground trying to remove his daughter from the cactus.

"Mmmmm," Téa mumbled between sobs.

"Hush baby, Daddy is here. Lord this is going to hurt," her father cried. "Jesus Christ, HELP!!!" he screamed. His sons arrived first, with their mother close behind. The oldest son, Antonio, sheltered her from seeing Téa like this. "Mother, you don't need to see her like this!" He was strong like his father, but still she almost broke through, "NO, NO, NO! NOT MY BABY!" Mother fought.

    It took an hour to separate Téa from the stubborn cactus and once home, it took hours to remove the large boney thorns. It took several more hours to remove the small yellow barbs that the larger thorns had implanted in her tender skin. Poor Téa bravely underwent the long sessions of painful removal of a thousand pricking needles. Mother and Lola, using small tweezers, patiently took turns removing the needle-like stickers that punished nearly every part of Téa's front body. After the removal of the barbs, the treatment continued with baths of alcohol several times a day to prevent infection that were required for a week. Sleeping, or at least trying to, was the worst.

    The doctor made daily visits, and friends kept the family's spirit up, but when the Monteros' housekeeper came to tell Téa's mother about her errant behavior, she got the surprise of her life. If she only had known that Téa's mother would not react accordingly, she most definitely would have left the fish and pee incident untold. Mrs. León had no tolerance for her daughter's mischievousness, but at this time she was worried for her daughter's life and didn't have the patience, nor the time, to bother with the snobbish woman and her complaints. She grabbed the younger woman by her collar, and without saying a single word, dragged her out of her house and up to the paved road. Mrs. León dropped the maid, took a deep breath, shook her apron, and said, "There!"

Embarrassed, the scorned maid stood up and left.

## CHAPTER NINE

# You Never Know

Téa was expected to spend some of her afternoons with Mrs. Milagros as long as she left the old lady's exotic plants alone. However, the cactus incident postponed the girl's visits a few months.

The worst part seemed to be behind her, and Téa was able to step out of bed for brief walks around the house. Mrs. León kept her daughter close by, cleaning her wounds and making sure her unwilling daughter didn't fall into trouble again.

"Go back to bed Téa," Mother said.

"But Mother, I'm bored!" Téa cried.

"Téa! Bed!" Mother shouted.

"I am, I am." Téa painfully tried not to limp. Nano ran to her side offering his arm, "I'm ok Nano."

"You want to see my rock collection?" he asked.

"As long as it doesn't have ants in it..." she tried to smile.

Téa carefully sat on her bed and slowly lifted her legs. Her brother covered her with the sheets. He sat on the foot of the bed and sighed. "So... are you going to show me your collection or what?" she asked.

"Oh yea!" he replied while nodding. The boy hopped off the bed to get the rocks out of his pockets. "Here!" Nano proudly produced three rocks and was busy rearranging them for his sister.

The rocks were identical. Téa waited a few seconds, "That's it?"

"Yep, that's all I got. I just started my collection this morning." Téa looked at her brother and smiled with pity. "Here, check this one out. It's kind of sparkly if you move it back and forth." Téa did what her brother asked.

"Isn't it pretty?" Téa humored him with a nod. "There, you can have it," Nano sang.

"Oh, no, that's ok!" She tried to give it back.

"Please keep it, I'm about to go back for more," he said as he picked the other two up and returned them to his pocket. "The sparkles will keep you entertained!" Nano left his sister, rock in hand. "Now you have a pet rock to look after," he said as he closed Téa's door.

"A pet rock?" Téa shook her head as she stared at the simple rock. Bored, she lay on her back and with both hands rotated her pet rock. "Ah, Nano, Nano. Only you could come up with something like that, a pet rock." she whispered.

"Knock, knock..." Mother said as she entered her daughter's room. "Look who came to see you!" Mrs. Varea had come to see her many times before, but Téa had always been asleep.

"Mrs. Varea?" Téa cried. "I thought you were dead!"

"Me, dead? Why would you think that?"

"Well, not just you, Mrs. Varea, your entire family too, including the dog." Téa said, "Your place looked as if everyone had vanished at the same time, in the middle of their chores. What spooked me the most was that when I called, no one answered."

"That's the day you fell on the cactus, right?" Mrs. Varea asked.

"Yes, unfortunately that was the day," Mrs. León answered. The flash back from that awful day gave her the willies all over her body.

"Yes, our dog died suddenly! Don't ask me why, or what he died of, because I don't know. All I know is that just in case it was something bad, we decided to bury him right away. My husband carried the poor beast as far as he could. Thank God for wheelbarrows!" she exclaimed.

Mrs. Varea's visit was short. Farm life was hard for everyone, especially for a family of four. She often said the twins were more trouble than they were worth.

"Well, I hate to run, but God knows what I'll find if I stay longer." She stood up and sighed. "I would kiss you, but I'm afraid I would hurt you." Téa thanked her. Mother walked her out and as soon as they finished with their small talk and goodbyes, she returned to check on Téa.

"Guess what I have behind my back?" Mrs. León sang to her convalescent daughter.
Téa shook her head, "What?"

"Your shoes!" her mother announced with irony. "I guess you left them there," she said as she placed them under the bed. The poor girl had her mouth wide open, but thankfully composed herself before her mother turned her face back to her. "You thought Mrs. Varea would never return them, right?" Téa was afraid to ask. "She brought your brother's too." Mrs. León seemed happy. "Now, no more walking barefoot. Is that clear young lady?"

"Yes, Mother," Téa responded. But to avoid eye contact, she pretended to study her pet rock.

"Where do you think you're going with all those rocks?" Mother said, wasting no time directing her son and his shirt full of small rocks outside. "There, set them free!" Mother ordered. Nano unwillingly threw them in a pile. *I'll get them later*, he thought as he walked away.

"If you know what's best for you, don't bring them back in the house," his mother announced. *How did she know what I was thinking*? Nano was convinced she could read minds. "And put your shoes on." Nano froze and his mother noticed. "Don't worry, Mrs. Varea brought them back, yours and your sister's. Try not to be so forgetful next time, alright?" his mother said with a smile. "They are under your sister's bed."

"Pssst, Téa..." Nano whispered from the door. Téa motioned to him to come closer with her hand.

"I know what you're thinking..."

"The Varea brothers!" Nano interrupted.

"Hush...before Mother hears us."

"Those two, I thought they liked us." Nano was mad.

"Well, we don't know how our shoes ended up in the hands of their mother, but until we do, we have to keep calm," Téa whispered.

"But, what about our clothes? If they took everything..." Nano whispered.

"Like I said, we just have to wait until I see those two..." Téa didn't have a chance to finish her sentence because her mother came back into the room. "Here, eat this." Mother left migote on the nightstand. "Let it set for a minute or two or you will burn your tongue." Nano came closer to smell the treat. "Nano yours is waiting in the kitchen," Mother announced. "Come on son, it's almost bed time," she said when she didn't see her son following her.

"Can I sleep with Téa?" he asked.

"That's up to your sister." Mother waited for Téa to response.

"Yes."

"Are you sure?"

"Yes Mother, I'm feeling so much better," Téa said in a reassuring tone. She was all smiles.

"Great, then tomorrow you will start your visits to Mrs. Milagros." Téa's smile vanished, but Nano couldn't help his. He was just so happy to be sleeping with his sister again.

The next morning Téa woke up and the first thing on her mind was breakfast, then she remembered that she had to pee. The bathroom was on the opposite side of the house, and you had to cross through the kitchen to get to it. Her breakfast was waiting for her. "I'm starving!" Téa announced as she passed by.

"Good morning to you too," Mother said.

"Yeah, Good morning," she said from the bathroom. "What's this?" Téa asked when she saw a dress about her size resting on a chair.

"That's for you to wear to see Mrs. Milagros."

"Over my dead body," she said with an attitude.

"Well, dead or alive you're wearing it," Mother said with a chuckle. "By the way, what happened to the pants and the shirt your cousin gave you?" Téa quickly changed her mind and put on the ugly dress.

"Well, well, look at you. It fits you perfectly!" Mother said proudly.

"Really Mother?" Téa said as she stood there with her sleeves hanging over her hands.

"Oh, just pull those sleeves up a little that's all," Mother said as she helped her daughter with some minor adjustments.

"When am I going to get clothes of my own? I'm sick and tired of hand-me-downs," Téa whined as her mother placed a short white apron over her waist so it would appear to fit better. "Aggg Mother not so tight, I can't breathe!"

"Ok, there now" Mother said as she made her daughter turn a few times. "Now you can go."

"What about breakfast?" Téa asked as if her mother was kidding. "You'll dirty your pretty dress, and we can't risk it." Mother pushed her out the door.

"But I'm hungry!" Téa complained as she drug her feet trying to stop her mother.

"Mrs. Milagros will feed you, and then you are free to stain it, but not before you present yourself to her."

Téa was mad, discontent and hungry... very hungry. *Ahhh and all because of this stupid dress. Look at me...I look hideous. What color is this dress anyway?* Téa's thoughts rambled on as she made her way to Mrs. Milagros' walking as if she were going to beat someone.

She arrived, and this time the gate opened easily. Téa cursed as if the gate were to blame for being unlocked. Téa was nervous. She had seen Mrs. Milagros before, and remembering her looks sent chills through her body. She seemed too cold for Téa's taste.

The old lady was sitting outside awaiting her guest at a picnic table ready for business. Mrs. Milagros was dressed in her usual mourning black. Her silver hair was combed perfectly and pulled straight back into a tight bun. Black is the color of sorrow, and Téa wondered who had died, but all those thoughts disappeared at the sight of the round table filled with pastries and a pot of hot chocolate. *If this is the way she teaches, I am in.* "Buenos dias," Téa said greeting her host.

Mrs. Milagros answered without moving her body. "Take a seat Téa," the old lady ordered the girl. Sitting there as she was, Mrs. Milagros reminded Téa of a statue. *I swear she must have a stick up her ass, how else could she keep her back that straight?*

A well-dressed maid offered Téa a chair next to the lady. Without so much as a look, Mrs. Milagros offered her a pastry from the tray. Téa grabbed it and without thinking twice, shoveled it into her mouth; all of it. Mrs. Milagros was horrified at Téa's manners and couldn't help but stare. The hungry girl stopped mid-munch, and with her mouth full managed to say, "What?" as crumbs fell out of her mouth. Mrs. Milagros said nothing. Instead, she gave her a white cloth to wipe her mouth. "Sorry Señora, did I do something wrong?" The old lady gave her a mischievous smile.

"I'm glad you asked, Téa. Today's first lesson will be on etiquette at the table."

"Etiqu...what?" Téa had no idea what that word meant.

*Since when eating had become some sort of an art?* Téa wondered.

Bored to tears, Téa listened to her new teacher, but at least she could eat at the same time.

All she could do was follow directions and stare back at the old woman's broach. It was large and bore her picture from her younger days. Mrs. Milagros wore it proudly pinned to her black silk blouse.

Téa kept comparing the woman to the picture. She noticed how her nose had grown larger, as well as her ears. Suddenly, her eyebrows visibly narrowed. Mrs. Milagros had finally smiled. Téa hesitated, but soon smiled back.

Mrs. Milagros gently took another pastry, placed it on a small saucer and handed it to her.

"Now, try again, but this time eat slowly and one bite at a time. No one is going to take it away," she said nicely.

Téa did what she had been told and took the cookie gently as instructed. In slow motion the cookie travelled to her mouth where she held it in place while opening her mouth even slower. Mrs. Milagros followed the cookie attentively, her eyes opening widely as Téa took the first slow bite. Mrs. Milagros's head slowly followed the motion of the girl's mouth shutting. Téa paused, waiting for more instructions.

"Well, well, nicely done Téa. Now chew it slowly," Mrs. Milagros instructed. The girl obeyed.

Téa thought she would be pleased, but obviously she was still doing something wrong. "Great Téa, you're doing great. Now, take another bite. A little faster this time...and don't forget to close your mouth with each and every bite, alright?" She smiled sourly again. Téa never thought in a million years she could ever be tired of eating cookies, but she was.

That was just breakfast; more practicing came with lunch.

*Who would have thought there was so much to learn about eating?*

Téa learned how to eat fish with a special fork and knife, that for soup you used a big spoon, and that desserts and coffee used a teeny tiny one.

So many rules. There were rules for everything. She certainly didn't care, but wanting to please Mrs. Milagros, she did as she was told.

## CHAPTER TEN

# Bitter Sweet

Three months had been invested into Téa's education, and so far they had covered nothing but table manners. However, Mrs. Milagros seemed happy with her improvements.

"Téa, which of the pastries do you favor the most?" Téa took a moment and when she thought she had a winner, she hesitated again.

"They are all good, aren't they? What a dilemma. But like I always say, there is a solution for every problem." Mrs. Milagros took a small fork and divided each pastry into four portions. "There, problem solved. Shouldn't all issues in life be this easy?" The old lady took a piece and Téa took another.

"These pastries came all the way from Sevilla, did you know that?" Mrs. Milagros discouraged the maid from pouring more coffee in her cup by placing her hand over it.

"I'm going to pay the nuns who bake them a visit very soon. Would you like to come along? You could watch how these delicious things are made while I conduct my business. What do you say?"

It sounded good at the time, so she gave her a quick nod. Téa was so excited to taste the small bites that she would have said yes to jumping into the abyss.

The day's lesson was over, and Téa took the few leftover cookies the maid had wrapped for her and left after kissing Mrs. Milagros' hand.

"And don't worry. Your parents already know," Mrs. Milagros sang. Téa politely nodded again.

The sun began to rise softly to its ultimate peak while a rooster made sure everyone knew. Téa's mother stormed into her daughter's room and pulled open the wooden drapes. "Téa get up! You don't want to be late. Get up Téa! The bath water is getting cold."

*Water? Bath?* Téa was convinced she was having a bad dream. Knowing Téa, her mother quickly pulled the covers down creating a wave of crisp air. Téa's warm body curled up even more. "Mother..." she whined. "Mmmm no, I'm tired. One more minute, pleaseeeee," Téa begged.

"No," Mother said. "Every morning Téa, every morning the same game, no matter how early, no matter how late, you always do this to me. Téa, get up! I warn you, your sister is coming with the bucket!" Téa knew her sister wouldn't hesitate to pour it on her. She sluggishly made it out of bed but complained all the way to the bathroom that she didn't deserve a bath.

"Are you serious? Mother! Please! I already had my bath for the week! I can't...so early...I'm cold!"

"You must look your best! Mrs. Milagros' chauffeur should be here any minute! You can't be late, that would be rude," Mother rambled.

"Can't I look good without getting wet?" Téa asked. Mother softly backhanded the back of her daughter's head and dryly said no. "Take your pajamas off and get in the water. NOW!"

"Alright, alright! No need to yell, I'll take the damn bath!"

Mother looked at her daughter with frustration, "And I want to see soap in that water, and please dry yourself well."

Just when Téa thought her mother was done, she added, "And wear a dress."

"I don't understand why I have to bathe, I don't care to impress anyone. It's not like I'm not going to get dirty again," Téa complained.

"Téa, next time I'll serve your food on a dirty plate, alright?" Mother said.

"I don't care," Téa answered nonchalantly while she stared at the bar of soap. "Again, I don't see the need."

"Can you just hush and wash?" Mother's tone meant business and Téa knew it, so she obeyed.

As mother predicted, Mrs. Milagros' chauffeur arrived early and was waiting patiently while reading his newspaper.

Téa's mother grabbed her arm, "Wait, wear this in your hair." Mother quickly pinned a small bow on Téa's head, having to rearrange the ugly looking thing on a chunk of hair.

"Behave!" her mother advised.

The chauffeur had his newspaper put away in no time. Like a good magician, he folded the enormous newspaper and tucked it under his arm. The car door was already open, and his hand reached out to help Téa with the high gap between the ground and the inside of the car. She hesitated, because his gloves look so pristine.

"Good morning, Téa. Let me help you." He said it so gently that the girl couldn't refuse.

Téa could care less about the luxurious car. It made her quite uncomfortable. The smell of leather overwhelmed her and soon her stomach was turning. Téa asked permission to roll the window down.

"Are you the kind who gets motion sickness?"

*I have no idea what he just said, but I better nod.* Téa was not used to fancy words.

They were running a little late, and Mrs. Milagros was already walking down the last few front steps. As soon as the car stopped, the chauffeur got out swiftly, leaving the roaring machine running with Téa inside.

The head maid was helping Mrs. Milagros carry her big purse while holding the car door open for her. The chauffeur returned out of breath with a handful of Jasmine. As Mrs. Milagros got settled, he placed half of the little perfumed flowers in the front with him and gave the rest to the girl. He did everything so quickly that of everyone there, Téa was the only one who noticed.

Mrs. Milagros' weak, old, languid body settled next to Téa's small, but robust body, making a sharp contrast when comparing the two.

"Miss Téa has something for you señora!" Téa looked at the chauffeur, then at the bunch of pleasant little flowers she held in her hands. The girl quickly put on a smile and gave them to the lady.

"How thoughtful! They are my favorite! Mr. Luna, I see you got some as well."

*Mr. Luna, so that's his name,* Téa thought. *His name matches his demeanor, seemingly cold at times but very gentle and bright. Yeah...like a full moon.* Téa kept smiling.

"Thank you, Téa!" sang the chauffeur with a big smile. Téa thanked him back.

Soon the three were on their way. It was a long three hour drive to the city of Sevilla, and thanks to the aromatic flowers Mr. Luna had generously provided, combined with the open windows, the anxious feeling that had made Téa's stomach turn, slowly began to dissipate. That and Mr. Luna's many gestures of kindness throughout the long trip. Yet, it was replaced by a feeling that was rapidly weighing down her heart. It was her first time away from home, and Téa missed her mother.

Téa had fallen asleep on Mrs. Milagros' lap, and she was dreaming of her mother. Her dream was so real that she could feel her mother's hand gently stoking her arm. It was Mr. Luna.

"Where's Mrs. Milagros?" Téa said in a raspy voice as she gave a long hard stretch.

"La señora is inside the convent; she thought you looked too angelic to wake you up."

"How long have I been asleep?" Téa yawned.

"Not too long," he answered as he opened his ABC newspaper.

"Then why did you wake me up? I'm ready to turn around and go home." Téa yawned again.

"Well, let's just say I couldn't concentrate on my reading."

"Why? Was I passing gas or something?" asked Téa with a smirk on her face.

"No, thank God, but you sure snore like an old man." He chuckled as he turned his page. Téa thought it was funny too.

At that particular moment a young nun softly knocked on the window. The chauffeur quickly laid his newspaper on the passenger's seat and got out of the car with a big smile.

Mr. Luna opened the door on Téa's side. "Téa, Sister Ana will take you to Mrs. Milagros." Téa didn't move. "Don't you want to go?" he asked.

"Not really," she said.

"Oh, come on. You'll get bored waiting here with me." Mr. Luna had half of his body in the back seat trying to reach for the girl. "I don't like nuns," Téa whispered.

"What? You don't like nuns?" he sang with a whisper. "Hey come on Téa, don't be that way, nuns are nice. They help people," he whispered with a serious face.

"They weren't nice to me or my little brother. Please let me wait here for Mrs. Milagros." Mr. Luna sighed and backed out.

"I'm sorry Sister, the poor girl isn't feeling well. Tummy troubles...," he said rubbing his knuckles. He did that with his hands every time he was being untruthful. "Too long of a trip I suppose," he continued.

"I'll tell Mrs. Milagros," she said. "Can I get you anything little one?" The religious woman peeked her head in the window while Téa clenched her torso with pain. Téa shook her head and whispered no. "Oh, poor thing...you look awful. I hope you feel better soon. I'll pray for you," Sister Ana said with a sad look.

"God bless you sir," she said before leaving.

Mr. Luna nodded and waved; somehow he felt guilty lying to a woman of God.

"See what you made me do?" he said to Téa as soon as it was safe.

"What? I made you do nothing," she said.

"Oh right, yeah, *I don't like nuns... I'm not going*...you left me no choice, just by the way you were acting. By the way, you were very convincing," he said snidely.

"Are you mad at me?" Téa said looking down at her hands.

"No, I'm not mad. I'm just too old for this sort of game," he said as he tapped the girl's hands. "Now, you better look sick for Mrs. Milagros." Téa suddenly began to push on her stomach. She looked like she was in pain. "Not now...!"

"Not now what?" asked Mrs. Milagros.

"Mrs. Milagros!" he jumped. "I need a bag! She's about to vomit!" He ran to the front to retrieve a paper bag from the glove compartment.

"Thank God, Mr. Luna. You're always so prepared. There, there..." the old woman said as she touched the girl's forehead.

"We can't stay," Mrs. Milagros said. "Mr. Luna I'm ready to head home." The old lady sat by Téa and closed the car door. She rolled the window half way down and apologized to Mother Superior for leaving so suddenly. "I'm so sorry Mother."

"No need to apologize my dear Señora, go in peace, and we hope little Téa will feel better soon. We'll have her in our prayers," the nun said.

"Mother, spare a few for me as well; I haven't been myself lately," Mrs. Milagros asked. Mr. Luna had his hand on the ignition key and was looking over his shoulder waiting for Mrs. Milagros to give him the ok.

"We have you in our prayers my dear Señora, always," Mother Superior said as she squeezed the old lady's hand. "Thank you for everything Mrs. Milagros, God Bless you!" With her free hand, the worried Mrs. Milagros gave a few dry taps on the car door, signaling she was ready to go.

CHAPTER ELEVEN

# Cookie Trap

"Mr. Luna, to Villa Rosa," Mrs. Milagros ordered.

"But, I thought we were on our way home," Téa said.

"We can't, a storm is coming, and you don't look too good," Mrs. Milagros said.

"But I'm feeling better, and a little rain never hurt anyone," Téa pleaded.

"I'm sorry Téa, but no." Mrs. Milagros dried her forehead and then her wrinkled neck. "Mr. Luna hurry up please, before it gets worse." Thunder made Mrs. Milagros more than ill.

The afternoon had grown sad, and the approaching night was not promising any peace.

"But I want to go home!" Téa screamed loudly.

"I want my mama!" Téa cried, and the old woman screamed too, not because of Téa's scream, but at a thunder crashing with fury over the moving car. Téa sobbed all the way to the house Mrs. Milagros had on the outskirts of Sevilla.

The ride took longer than normal because Mr. Luna had to take a detour twice because of the flooded roads.

It was dark, very dark, and to keep from running off the road, Mr. Luna had to push on the brakes from time to time, which jerked the unsuspecting back passengers violently. He would apologize and wait for the bright lightening to lead the way again.

Meanwhile Téa screamed at the top of her lungs, "We're going to die!" while Mrs. Milagros hid between the seat's gap holding her oversize bag over her head.

"Please Mr. Luna, do you see the house yet?" asked Mrs. Milagros from her uncomfortable safe-hole.

"No, señora."

Mrs. Milagros repeated the same question over and over while Téa wished she was home.

Miraculously they reached their destination. The car came to a stop and no one waited for anyone. Mrs. Milagros opened her door as the butler quickly made his way around just in time. Téa hung to the old lady as if it were raining acid. The scared bundle ran inside covered by the umbrella while the butler got soaked. Mr. Luna drove the car around to the back.

The entry to the house was open to sky high ceilings causing their steps to echo each time they moved. The room beyond the entry was big and cold as well. One of the maids was trying to remedy the problem by lighting a fire in the stone fireplace.

They were definitely in for the night, and as much as Téa missed her mother and hated to be in a strange house; she accepted her fate with resignation.

Mrs. Milagros painstakingly threw herself on one of the large chairs close to the fire. One look at her and you would think she had walked all the way from the convent. "Maria, the stool." The maid obeyed, placing the small piece of furniture under her master's feet.

"Should I remove your shoes, Señora?" the maid asked. Mrs. Milagros nodded and leaned her head back and sighed tiredly.

"Maria, bring me a drink and my pill for thunders." Mrs. Milagros named her entire female staff Maria and only used their real name if she fancied them.

"Let me show you to your room, Señorita," said one of the maids. The girl looked at Mrs. Milagros for guidance, but the old lady had her eyes closed. "Mrs. Milagros?" Téa sounded intimidated. The old lady, eyes still shut, waved her hand in a lazy dismissal. The maid gently pushed the unwilling girl towards the door. The maid took the lead as soon as they left the room, and after climbing the steps of the giant staircase, the girl, breathing heavily, grabbed the end of the wood rail, and huffed, "Just a moment." The maid waited, but not for long. She walked towards the room closest to the staircase and entered. Téa followed her, leaving the door wide open.

"Whoa, whoa! What are you doing? I think I can manage to do this on my own!" Téa didn't know what to think when the maid began to undress her.

The poor maid removed her hands from the girl faster than if she had touched a burning stove. The maid, far from looking upset, apologized to her. Téa thought of her mother's submissive ways when around Mrs. Milagros. She felt bad.

"That's alright, I'm sorry, I just didn't expect to be touched," Téa said.

*If she only knew I was just like her,* she thought.

Téa was left alone with the gigantic bed so high it had a stool placed on the side for easy access. A long white camisole rested on the foot of the bed for her. The room had a musky smell that made her miss her mother even more. Happy that no one forced her to take a bath, she undressed and was soon wearing the ugly camisole. She tucked herself into the cold bed missing the warmth of her little brother.

The dark room flashed with blinding light announcing the deafening blast of thunder. The strong winds blew the pounding rain into the windows like thousands of impertinent woodpeckers. Téa usually loved to sleep to the sound of rain, but this was way too much. Making matters worse, if you paid attention, you could hear a woman's cry during each fading of the thunder's crash, but only if you paid attention. The girl was sure she wouldn't sleep at all that night, but somehow between tossing and turning, the last thing Téa remembered was closing her eyes and wishing for a pleasant sleep. Sleep makes time go faster, and before she knew it, the girl was covering her eyes from the morning sun that was beating in the window with vengeance. She smiled.

Happy she was going home, Téa wanted to dress and be on her way. She was upset her clothes were gone and automatically blamed the maid. A soft knock stopped her search as the maid from last night entered the room.

"Your bath is ready Señorita," the maid said politely. With one hand she held the door open, and with the other directed her to the bathroom.

"I'm sorry, but no bath for me today," Téa announced as she resumed looking for her clothes.

"And why is that?" the maid asked.

"Well, I can't find my clothes for one, and two, I hate baths." The maid stood by the door in silence.

"I would appreciate it if you helped me look," Téa said.

"No need, la Señora has taken care of that. Your new clothes are waiting by the bath."

When Téa saw the clothes resting on a chair, she quickly picked them up with two fingers and pointed them at her, "It's not my size." She was convinced.

"Really? Mm I'm sure that dress will fit you, Señorita. Your own mother gave Mrs. Milagros your measurements, or at least that's what la Señora said when she showed me the note.

"My mother didn't write it."

"And why are you discussing this with me? Just get in the water and quit squandering my time."

Téa was left alone.

"Wow, look at this! It looks like a pool!" Téa exclaimed.

Téa didn't mind bathing in this tub. It was big enough for two full size adults, unlike the small tin bucket that barely covered her waist and left her legs exposed to the cold air.

Here the water was crystal clear, and she could see the steam floating in the air. Téa tested the water first with her finger, "perfect temperature." Slowly she stepped in with both feet, then sat in the strange and wonderful bathtub. Resting on the side was an expensive loofa. She held it with curiosity and dropped it in the water. As it floated away from her, Téa inspected her surroundings and slowly sank her entire body in the hot water.

She comfortably settled herself and stared at the loofa slowly navigating towards her feet. She tried to retrieve it with her feet, pulling it slightly towards her, but it kept gravitating to the same place, her feet. Feeling too lazy to move, she had the bright idea to rock her body back and forth. *Well done!* she thought.

It wasn't long before the loofa was dancing all over the bathtub. Téa was having a great time as the water splashed all over the floor, "Ah, the perfect storm!" she whispered while making the sound of the wind and the splashing of the waves with her mouth.

"You are lucky Mrs. Milagros has a tender heart, because if it was up to me your bratty ass would be drowned this very moment." The soft spoken maid somehow didn't sound the same. Her voice made Téa freeze at once but the water continued splashing with a life of its own. The maid placed several large white towels on the floor and handed one to Téa as she waited for her to get out of the tub.

"Get dressed; la Señora is waiting for you. Please hurry, the nuns will be here any minute now, and they don't like to waste time." The maid smiled. Téa felt chills as she rose up from the water.

She remembered the cookies that the nuns made, and the thought awakened her growling tummy. With that in mind, Téa dressed in her new clothes and was on her way faster than you can say "Cookie."

Téa opened the bathroom door to find the annoying maid sitting in a small chair waiting for her.

"Follow me," the maid ordered as she stood up.

Téa remembered the sounds of the night before and asked the maid, "Who was crying last night?"

She thought some small talk would soften the edges between them, but the maid didn't answer, at least right away.

"I can't say I heard anything but thunder and rain," she finally said as she calmly increased her pace. Téa sensed the maid had probably had enough of her.

The maid stopped in front of two large wood and glass doors, straightened her uniform, and then held open one of the doors for the young señorita. Normally Téa would have felt extremely uncomfortable with all the pomposity surrounding the magnificent architecture, but it seemed that all the time spent at Mrs. Milagros' bigger than life house helped her act unimpressed and natural.

Mrs. Milagros was seated at the breakfast table as two maids dressed in white made the finishing touches on the table settings. She smiled at Téa, which made the girl nervous. Mrs. Milagros was never that enthusiastic. Téa guessed that like an old motor, she probably just needed time to warm up.

"Good morning, Téa!"

"Good morning, Señora!"

"I hope you were able to sleep with the storm and all." Her hand trembled as she held her coffee cup.

"Oh! Bad weather never bothered me much, but... that cry, am I the only one who heard it?" Mrs. Milagros' hands shook even more nervously. She had to use both hands to hold her cup.

"No...I can't say that I did," she answered.

"Señora, Mother Superior has just arrived." One of the servants barely had time to make the announcement before Mother Superior, wearing her full black and white habit, entered the room and rushed towards the breakfast table like she had obviously done it many times before; a box of cookies in hand.

"My dear friend, always so punctual. Please sit," Mrs. Milagros said joyfully as she kissed her hand.

"Coffee?" said Mrs. Milagros. The nun nodded as she gave the box to one of the maids closest to her.

The nun looked straight into Téa's eyes and as she took her seat, proudly stated, "Punctuality is the soul of business." Téa had an uneasy feeling in her stomach. "Black, no sugar," the religious woman added without looking at the maid who was pouring the coffee.

*Business? Ah! Yes...the cookies,* Téa remembered.

"So...finally I get to meet the nice young lady you've been telling me about." The nun examined Téa from head to toe.

*Nice? Me?* Téa was confused.

She had never been complimented before, so Téa was searching the room for this other girl.

As soon as she realized that she was talking about her, she stood up, reached for the nun's hand and pretended to kiss it in the same fashion she had seen in the movies. Mother Superior pulled away before Téa could recreate the scene, leaving her lips kissing the air.

"Maria! We need privacy; show Téa to the library."

*But, what about the cookies?* Téa wanted breakfast.

Téa obeyed, and with disdain followed one of the many maids named Maria. To her relief there was a breakfast table waiting for her. A large plate of warm churros and hot chocolate. *Much better,* Téa thought.

Blind with hunger, she rapidly took her seat and proceeded to binge.

"Just one moment!" the maid interrupted.

*Of course, it was too good to be true,* she thought.

The maid shook out the white linen napkin and placed it over the girl, almost covering her entire body. "We can't take any chances," the maid said as she pulled Téa's sleeves up. "Here, before you start making a mess, grab that box." The maid pointed to a pretty wooden box that decorated the table. It was very fancy, carved with exquisite detail.

"Very pretty!" Téa humored her hoping to be left alone with the churros.

"No...open it, there is something inside for you," the maid said as she pushed the box closer to Téa.

Téa did not expect any presents and was now definitely surprised, especially since the box wasn't wrapped and she had thought it was there for decoration.

She opened it to discover a gold wrist watch. Impressed, Téa's mouth gaped open. She took it out of the box and easily slid the stretch band over her wrist. The maid finally left her alone.

Téa stared at the beautiful piece as she dipped churros in the hot chocolate.

*I'm sure she must be waiting to hear my reaction,* Téa thought.

She took the oversized napkin off, grabbed a few churros and ate them on her way.

Mrs. Milagros' room wasn't too far, and sinceshe still had a mouthful of churros, she stood outside the room trying to swallow the big bites. Téa couldn't wait to show her gratitude. That's when she overheard Mother Superior explaining to Mrs.

Milagros that it was in the girl's best interest to enroll her in their boarding school right away. Téa dropped her churros and ran back to where she was supposed to be.

*Over my dead body!* She thought as she pulled off the expensive watch and just stared at the hot chocolate.

Téa had lost her appetite.

"What's the matter now? You're full already?" The maid complained as she entered the room.

"Child, you're pale as a ghost." Téa looked at her but said nothing.

## CHAPTER TWELVE
# The Tantrum

Téa's chest burned with anxiety as she waited for the bossy nun to leave. She knew the well-intentioned Mrs. Milagros would try to persuade her to enter the good school, but all Téa wanted to do was to go home. The poor girl looked at the plate of churros where nothing but a few crumbs remained. *Did I eat them all?* She realized she must have eaten them compulsively out of fear while waiting. The thought of never seeing her family again controlled her mind.

"Téa, la Señora wants you," another Maria said from the door.

Téa stood up, and her stomach turned. "Are you ok?" For once the maid looked genuinely concerned.

The girl nodded, but apparently she wasn't very convincing. The maid came to her side with her apron ready in case she got sick. "I can't believe you ate them all," she kept repeating as Téa tried not to vomit. The girl felt as if the hallway to the breakfast room had become painfully longer. Téa didn't remember arriving, nor did she remember sitting down. All she remembered was trying to make out Mrs. Milagros' blurry face when all hell broke loose. Téa vomited; followed by a ringing in her ears and a momentary feeling of relief. Once again Téa found herself in trouble, but this time she wanted to die.

Téa thought as long as she continued to vomit, Mrs. Milagros would maybe feel sorry for her and possibly let this one slide. Téa kept on and on even though there was nothing else inside her.

"Here drink this," Mrs. Milagros said with a sour face.

Téa shook her head no, but she insisted. "Take a sip, just one, it's warm and it'll do you good. It will settle your stomach."

Téa knew exactly what that brew was...*tila,* the same nasty old tila. Mother gave it to her every time she ate too much. Téa should be used to the taste by now, but she still disliked it

"Can I go home?" Téa asked.

"Take a sip and we'll see!" Téa took one hoping Mrs. Milagros would say yes.

Téa was surprised by the first sip, it tasted good. Téa gulped the hot drink down all at once. "Can I go home now?"

"Not today, you're too sick for traveling. We'll see how you feel tomorrow." Mrs. Milagros said.

The maid was standing by the sickly girl and soon was lifting Téa out of the chair. She was as strong as a mountain, and it took no effort to carry Téa to her room.

The maid slid the sick girl onto the bed and rushed to lower the blinds. She came back to Téa's side and stood there in silence.

"What?" Téa snapped.

"Isn't the señorita going to take her clothes off?" the maid said with a certain air of deviousness.

"Yes, I can do that all by myself. Thank you." Téa sounded bitter.

"Listen girl, I want you gone as bad as you want to be gone, but in the meantime why don't you lose that attitude?"

"Well, if I'm not on my way home by tomorrow, I, I..."

"You'll what? You'll run away?" the maid chuckled.

Not knowing how to respond, Téa slowly began to undress while the maid lifted the large pillow. "Here." The maid gently removed Téa's nightgown from the night before and placed it at the foot of the bed. "I'll be sitting right outside your door in case you need me," the maid said before closing the door. Téa heard a key locking the door from the outside.

Téa spent the day in bed waiting for the next morning to arrive. When tomorrow finally came, Téa had been dressed and ready to go since before the sun came up. Tired of waiting, she thought she would make noise by playing with the door knob, but the door opened with just one turn of the wrist.

*I could have sworn I heard this door being locked.*

Slowly she tip-toed to where she heard voices outside. It was Mr. Luna talking to the maid as he prepared Mrs. Milagros' automobile. Téa didn't care what their conversation was about, as long as she was going home.

*I knew it! I'm going home!*

Happy, Téa couldn't help but to do a little dance from time to time as she walked towards the entrance.

"There you are!" Mr. Luna sang.

Téa waved with a smile as she wished a good morning to the more familiar face of Mr. Luna.

The maid smiled and wished good morning back. Téa gave her a suspicious look at the same time as she felt the wind of Mrs. Milagros' fan waving behind her.

"Come on Téa, I thought you wanted to leave?" Mrs. Milagros said with a hint of annoyance in her voice.

Téa rushed to the opened car and jumped in so forcefully that the car rocked from side to side.

Mr. Luna closed the door after he helped Mrs. Milagros get settled and was soon in his front seat ready to drive anywhere his boss lady ordered him.

Téa was all smiles when she looked at Mrs. Milagros. The old lady didn't look at her. She looked sad.

*It's not my fault she doesn't have a daughter of her own. I have a mother, and once you have one you can't give her back. It's too late, because you already love her.*

"Do you love your mother?" Mrs. Milagros asked.

"Of course I love my mother!"

"Exactly! It is something that comes naturally, and you just can't help it, right? Love is unconditional! You will understand when you get older..."

Téa wasn't sure where the old woman was going with all this talk of love, mothers, and grown up stuff.

*Old people...go figure* Téa thought, while appearing to seem interested.

The old lady went on, "Believe it or not, I was once young and in love. In love with someone my family didn't approve of, but who can choose who they love? No matter how obedient I was, and how much I prayed to become the daughter they wanted me to be, they still didn't approve. Well, youth just doesn't know any better, and tend to follow the yet untamed heart." The lady looked at Téa to make sure she was paying attention.

"The object of my affection was the son of our head gardener. I knew deep inside that what I felt for him was impossible, and if he hadn't returned my feelings I could have forgotten him; unfortunately that wasn't the case. My parents noticed our playful exchanges, and I was placed on a short leash. My father ordered my mother to follow me everywhere."

"So what happened?" Téa was sincerely interested.

The old lady rested her head back and sighed, "For a while it worked; my mother faithfully followed my father's instructions. Day after day I wouldn't talk. My mother let it go because, as she told me later, she understood I was upset. My mother would bring her Bible on our long walks, and when we grew tired we would stop under a good tree. I always had my diary with me, so I wrote and she read.

Eventually my mother would rest her eyes while the relaxing caress of the wind against the tree limbs and the chirps of the little birds made the perfect lullaby. Soon she would join the birds with her snoring.

Mother never noticed that the son of the gardener followed us." Mrs. Milagros paused for a moment.

"Did you get to spend time with him?" Téa asked with curiosity.

"Indeed I did. Silent time, but nevertheless fruitful with passion." The old woman had to pause again, her voice weakening.

"Did your mother ever discover your meetings?" Téa asked.

"Not to my knowledge. All I know is that one day the head gardener was dismissed, along with his son. I had my suspicions that father was involved. I never got to see him again." Mrs. Milagros rapidly pulled her handkerchief from her sleeve and patted her face with it.

Before Téa could ask more questions, the car stopped.

"We have reached our destination my lady," Mr. Luna announced.

"Thank you, Mr. Luna," Mrs. Milagros answered softly as she pulled herself together.

"Are we getting more cookies?" Téa asked naively.

"Yes, more cookies," the old woman said. "If you stay in this school, you can receive a good education...and you can have all the cookies you wish," she said cheerfully.

"Stay here?" Téa sounded panicky, but she quickly locked her eyes with Mrs. Milagros in a dead stare.

"Dear, are you alright? Say something..."

The old lady had not finished her sentence when Téa blasted out with a loud, "*HELL NO!*"

The nuns helped Mrs. Milagros with the stubborn girl and were pulling Téa by the arm, but the young girl kept escaping. A few more Godly women grabbed the girl, this time from both sides. Téa, feeling ambushed, forgot the few good manners she had learned, and as if possessed by the devil himself, began to scream obscenities at the nuns; but it didn't work. These nuns were tough. Téa began to spit on them, but the nuns didn't flinch. That's when the girl remembered how her little brother had won a wrestling fight against one of the Varea boys. Like a rabid dog, she began to bite everything that came in contact with her mouth. Soon she was free and running in the opposite direction. However, she didn't get very far. The younger nuns ran after her and managed to catch her before she could run away.

Téa cried and screamed as she was being pulled. "STOP!" said a voice.

It was Mrs. Milagros, "Let her go!"

The nuns reluctantly released the puffing girl.

Mrs. Milagros held Téa in her arms and said to her, "No need to run, I'm taking you home."

The old lady had Mr. Luna carry Téa to the car. He gently closed the car door behind them.

"Obviously you'll come back when you're ready," Mrs. Milagros said.

"Never," Téa whispered between sobs. Her soul was tired. The old lady had her purse open, and her hand was on the wristwatch box. She was ready to give it back to Téa, but paused at the girl's words.

"Then...never it is." Mrs. Milagros dropped the small box from her hand and tossed her purse aside. Neither spoke again on the entire trip to Téa's home.

CHAPTER THIRTEEN

# Boris Karloff

Téa was back home with her family, and the bad experience of her stay with Mrs. Milagros had become a thing of the past. Only occasionally did she have nightmares. They would make her jump up in bed with fear. Breathing hard, she would sink back under the covers and hold her little brother close. He would hold her back and whisper, "It's ok Téa, you are here to stay." Téa held him even harder.

One morning during breakfast there was a knock on the open door followed by a loud *Good Morning!* from Uncle Antonio as he let himself in. He was her mother's brother.

He stopped by early to show them a puppy he had found on his way to work. He was hoping his sister would keep it until he returned from work that evening. The puppy was about four months old, and looked like a mix between a beagle and a sheep dog.

Téa was the first to run for the pup. Once she saw the puppy's furry face and her shiny, perfectly round chocolate eyes, she grabbed it from her uncle without asking and squished it into her face. The puppy licked her and Téa giggled, "I love puppy breath!" Without saying another word she turned around and with the puppy in a bundle, left breakfast and everyone else behind.

"I'm glad I am not imposing on anyone," Uncle Antonio said with a chuckle.

"There, there... go. The pup is in good hands," his sister said.

"Téa wait for me!" interrupted Nano, who abruptly ran after his sister.

Their uncle smiled. "Thanks sis," he said. "By the way, the pup is a bitch. I believe with proper training she'll become an excellent shepherd dog," he said as he lit a cigarette. "Bitches learn faster." He chuckled, coughing from the smoke.

"You're always trying to be funny," she said as she slapped his back a few times.

Téa had never felt as happy as she did when she played with the puppy. For the first time since her return, she didn't think once about her terrifying ordeal. Excited with her new found friend, the young girl wasn't even thinking about what she loved most, *food*. Téa's mother watched her child transform from sad to vibrant the moment the puppy entered the room.

Happy, their mother prepared a basket with two bocadillos and some figs.

"Kids come," she sang while walking towards the shade of a lonely almond tree.

Téa held the puppy in her arms and walked towards her mother with Nano glued to her side insisting it was his turn to hold the puppy. It really was.

"Téa, aren't you hungry?" Mother laid out a small blanket for the picnic she had so lovingly prepared at home.

"I am!" Nano answered for her.

"Well eat something and don't forget to bring the basket back when you are finished." Téa nodded her head, eyes still fixed on her puppy.

Téa grabbed her bocadillo and to Nano's surprise, gave the pup the first bite, Nano looked at his meal and without giving it a second thought took a monster bite. As he munched with his mouth open, he used his two fingers to parade a miniscule piece of bread in front of the puppy, expecting it to leave his sister. It didn't happen.

"Let me have her," Nano said, now trying to lure the pup with a piece of meat.

"Not yet," she said as her brother gained the animal's attention.

"Not fair, let him go!" Téa had the dog pinned.

"I'm always last. You're never going to let me hold her!" Whining, his chin trembled and his small eyes threatened to burst with tears.

Téa looked at him and thought about how many nights she had longed for her sweet little brother, and now she was being selfish.

"Here, you're right. It has been your turn for a long while." Téa let the pup go.

"Easy! Easy! She's very fragile!" Téa loosened her brother's tight embrace.

"Ooh ooh sorry!" He gently let up on his grip and so did she. Téa watched them play as she slowly savored her tasty meal.

The afternoon flew by, and they were having so much fun that not only did they forget to bring back the empty basket, they almost forgot to return themselves.

"Look at those two young scamps!" Téa's mother said.

"Tito!" Téa ran to him.

"Oh! Tito Antonio, you're not coming for her, are you?" Téa said after she gave him a strong hug.

"Please Tito, can we keep her?

"Please!" the two sang in unison. "She is so perfect for us, please, Tito, please?" Téa whined.

Their uncle lit another cigarette with the end of his old one. "Well..." He looked at his sister and smiled with relief. "It's up to your mother..." His sister shifted her head in one swift nod and gave him the evil eye. "What do you say, Sis?" His smile disappeared, hoping his sister would say no and leave him guilt free and looking wonderful. He had done that to her since they were kids.

Mad, she smiled, "Sure, you can keep the puppy." Her brother smiled shaking his head.

"Sorry ki...what?" He had not seen this one coming. "But what about your husband? He's not going to like it Sis, not asking for his blessing." He thought that would be enough to persuade his sister.

"My dear little brother, you underestimate me way too often," she said.

"But I already had plans...!"

"Well, make other plans," his sister said as she walked him out.

"Certain dogs are only good for working, and this mix breed happened to be perfect for nothing but chaperoning sheep," he argued.

"Didn't you say bitches learn faster?" she said slyly. He left puffing.

"Now, this puppy is your responsibility Téa," Mother said as soon as she returned from giving her brother a lesson. "Consider her your birthday and Christmas gift from me and your father.

"She's mine too!" Nano cried. Mother sighed, "Yes son, she's yours too," their mother said as she patted his head.

"Nano, we have to come up with the perfect name. Let's go, we have a lot of thinking to do." The two left their mom behind with the pup.

For the next two days, Téa and Nano spent every minute of every day trying to come up with a name that would suit her well.

"Why don't you both give it a rest? This endless naming of the puppy is driving me crazy." Mother was mending a few garments and the thread was tangled. "It's Saturday, why don't you take your brother to the movies?" she said without taking her eyes off her needle work.

"But Mother! I..."

"It wasn't a question, Téa." Mother took a few coins from a handkerchief she had bundled up in her brassiere. "Here, you should have enough for tickets and some hard candy or a small bag of sunflower seeds. And the puppy stays..." Téa reluctantly exchanged the coins for the pup and they soon were on their way. Mother shook her head as she waved good bye.

"Now, now...here you are my little cutie," she cooed with the puppy. It was kind of comical.

"Nano, what film do you think they're playing?" Téa asked absentmindedly. Her mind was with her puppy.

"Mm, don't know, but hoping for a Boris Karloff," Nano said.

The cinema was only as far as the beach. They had not even made it to the theater yet when they saw a line of kids already forming on the sidewalk. "Are you kidding me?" Téa said, sounding annoyed.

"Is this the line to buy tickets?" Téa asked to no one in particular.

"Yeah! Haven't you heard? It's a new Karloff movie," said one of the kids in line.

Téa kept walking.

"Téa, we passed the end of the line," Nano said whining.

"Forget it. We'd never make it." Téa walked with determination. Nano knew what that meant, no waiting in line.

She held Nano's hand while the others in line yelled, "Hey, get in line!" Nano nervously sang the name of his favorite actor repeatedly the whole way to the ticket booth, "Boris Karloff, Boris Karloff...I'm gonna watch a movie of Boris Karloff, Boris Karloff," helping him ignore the angry kids.

Téa approached the first person in line. "Excuse me! But my mother, who was a few rows before you, just realized she was short a ticket," she explained.

"Oh! Hello Téa." It was one of the Varea boys. "Sure, go ahead," he said, quickly pushing the line back.

"Two please," Téa said politely to the same old guy that had been selling the tickets all of her life. The old fart knew Téa's maneuver. He had seen it done many times before, but, he could care less who was first in line as long as he sold all the tickets.

"You're welcome!" the Varea boy sang with a hint of annoyance as Téa left, ignoring him.

"Oh! Thank you, thank you." Téa winked at him making a clicking sound with her mouth, the same one she used for rushing her donkey.

"Smarty pants," the boy said under his breath as he shook his head.

"Come on Nano, let's get a good seat," Téa said, pulling him by his shirt.

"What about candy?" Nano stopped.

"First we want to find a good spot, you know. How many times do we have to go over this?" Téa sped up as she spotted the perfect seats.

"Ahhh! Yeah I knew that." Obediently, he followed his sister.

"Stay here, don't you go wandering off or..."

"I know, I know...or you'll eat my candy too." Nano interrupted.

"Worse, I won't let you play with the puppy." Téa placed her jacket on her seat and left.

Téa was back in a flash as the candy stand wasn't crowded yet.

"Here," Téa passed her brother's bag to him.

Nano thanked her and opened his candy's wrapper. "Not yet, wait for the movie to start or you'll be done before the middle of the film, and I don't have money to buy more." The cinema was rapidly filling with loud children.

The sweet smell of candy mixed with the salty scent of sunflower seeds was overwhelmingly inviting.

"Oh, what the heck. Do whatever you want," said Téa...mostly because she couldn't resist opening hers. Surprisingly Nano left his alone.

The lights dimmed and the loud voices were soon replaced by some of the grownups hushing the children.

The big screen soon switched from dark to glowing with the black and white image of planet earth with a single engine propeller making its way around the world. There was complete silence in the auditorium as the barely detectable sound of the plane flying around the globe gradually grew into normal range.

Loud music roared as the name of the main character showed in big, all capital letters across the big screen, *Boris Karloff* playing the creature monster in "Bride of Frankenstein." Everyone cheered. It was going to be a great event. You could feel the excitement in the air. Each and every soul present kept their eyes glued to the silver screen, relying on their sense of touch to keep track of their goodies.

The two hour movie went on with full audience participation, outcries, shrieks, excited clapping, various clatters and kids bustling in and out of their seats with fear. Regardless of how scared they were, no one dared leave the theater, seemingly wanting more of that thrill.

Inevitably the movie ended and the thrill was over. It was time to get out of their hard wood seats and leave fantasy land.

Téa, who was so quick and smart about getting in to the theater, had no choice but to wait her turn to leave.

Exiting the theater after nearly two hours in the dark was kind of funny. It was like everyone seemed to have been awakened from a long nap, and they were all chatting excitedly about their incredible dream.

"I couldn't get over the reaction of Frankenstein's bride when she first laid eyes on him. She sounded like a scared cat," Téa said with an air of disappointment. "I was so hoping for a happy ending."

Nano was not listening. He was jumping around the sidewalk singing a tune he had just made up, "Boris Karloff, Boris Karloff, Boris, Boris, Boris Karrrrr-lofffff!"

"You're getting on my nerves with your singing, Nano."

Nano paused for a brief moment, looked at his sister, smiled, and kept on going like nothing registered.

"I'll race you home!" Téa had not seen that one coming, but decided she was not going to pass her little brother.

"I win, I win!" Nano sang out loud with excitement. "I get to play with the puppy first!"

"Okay, okay you got it kiddo," Téa said acting as if she were out of breath.

They walked in to find the puppy sleeping pleasantly right by mother's side while she was snapping away at a mountain of peas.

"Shhhh quiet, she's been chasing the baby goat since you left."

"Bummer, I wanted to play with her," Nano said disappointed.

"Come sit with me and help me with these peas. You too, Téa," Mother whispered.

"I'm hungry," Téa said.

"Here, take my seat while I prepare you a plate."

"I'm hungry too!" Nano blurted out.

Mother smiled and left to get them some food, while the room filled with the cricking sound of peas being snapped. Nano began to sing his Boris song. "Have you thought any more about a name for our pup?" Téa said, annoyed.

"Boris Karloff!" he exclaimed.

"We can't call her Boris Karloff."

"Yes we can," Nano insisted.

"Do I need to remind you that Boris is a boy name? And she is a girl," Téa explained.

"Boris, I want Boris!" Nano was chewing on a green pea. Téa sighed, she was tired of arguing.

*Mmm, I guess Boris could be used as a girl's name...after all she is a dog,* she thought.

Téa was about to agree when Nano started again with the same tune, "I want Bori, Bori, Bori, Boriiiiii..."

"Okay fine! You win." Nano couldn't hear his sister. He was too busy with his tune.

"I want Bori, I want Boriiiii...!" He now had a bunch of green peas dancing around in his mouth.

"OKAY!!!" Téa screamed. Nano and his mouth froze. Téa spoke with a calmer voice. "We'll name her *Bori*, no *S*. Take it or leave it." Nano quickly gave her a nod.

## CHAPTER FOURTEEN

# Fair Weather

Six months passed and Bori had almost grown to her adult size, beautiful with healthy long soft hair. Téa loved to stroke it every chance she got.

The loyal dog followed her everywhere, leaving Nano sulking with jealousy.

"You always make her go with you," Nano cried.

"Really, Nano? Is that even possible? I don't even have her on a leash. Bori follows who she wants to." Téa was walking in front with Bori, and Nano followed closely behind. Nano was mocking what she said and making faces behind his sister's back.

"Come here Bori, Bori, you are my little Bobo." Nano leaned over and petted her as he walked beside her.

"Bobo?" Téa asked surprised.

"Short for Bori, silly." Nano said talking like a baby. "I named her, remember?"

"If you keep changing her name, you're going to confuse her," Téa advised.

"Nu-uh, she knows Bobo is like Bori but with a stutter." They both laughed and Nano felt good.

"I guess you're right, she's pretty smart." Téa rubbed her knuckles over her brother's soft head making him release his grip.

He tried to ride on Bori's back. "Nano leave her alone, you're going to hurt her! Hold my hand you silly boy and hurry up. Mother wanted us home an hour ago." Téa grabbed him by his shirt and successfully clutched his hand.

As soon as they spotted their house, they could see Mother's silhouette waving at them. "I wonder why she wants us home so early?" Nano said.

"I don't know, but Dad wouldn't have taken the trouble to tell us to be home unless it was important. We better obey, or..."

"Or he'll shave our heads," Nano quipped. Téa meant to say, 'or else' but since her little brother had already stated the obvious, she just laughed nervously and gripped his hand harder.

"Téa, hurry up!" Mother yelled. The two siblings were running now.

"Mrs. Milagros, it's Mrs. Milagros!" Mother sounded worried.

Téa went in with her mother and Nano stayed outside to play with Bori.

"What about Mrs. Milagros?" Téa asked defensively.

"Mrs. Milagros isn't feeling all that good these days you know; she looks so sad...it breaks my heart every time I leave her house. It wouldn't hurt you to visit her every now and again...after all..."

"After all she has done for me?" Téa interrupted.

"If you know what's best for you little girl, you will not be insolent with me. You think your father went haywire on you?" Téa was surprised by her mother's words.

"Alright, alright. I'm sorry Mother. I keep forgetting she was the one who stopped the nuns from taking me in," she said patting Mother's hands.

"She misses you," Mother said calmly. "And you know she wants what's best for you."

"I know, I know." Téa rolled her eyes. "But..."

"But nothing, tomorrow afternoon you are coming with me to keep her company while I pick some fruit for her. Did you hear me missy?"

"Yes, Mother."

Téa went outside to find Nano trying to teach Bori how to sit.

"Bori, sit!" Nano instructed again and again. Boris just stared at his hand going up and down.

"Sit, Bori, sit." He was now pushing Boris' lower back down. The puppy would move just enough to make Nano's hand slide, then raise her hind end back up like a spring.

Téa shook her head and went back inside. "Mother, can I have some of that stale bread?" Téa already had her hand in the bread sack.

"Only one piece, you know it takes me forever to fill that bag...with so many mouths to feed," Mother complained without taking her eyes off her dishes. "One piece, I said! You hear?" she yelled. Téa dropped the second piece back into the sack. *I swear the woman must have eyes in the back of her head.* Téa was too innocent to realize that her mother didn't need eyes where they didn't belong, she need only take a quick look at her daughter's reflection in the glass on the pantry door.

She broke the small bread piece into little chunks, as many as she could, and placed them in her pocket, hiding one in her hand which she closed in her fist. Nano was still going at it and growing impatient. "Sit, sit, sit! Bori, Bori come on... sit! sit!" Bori was not a bit interested.

"Wasting your time?" Téa laughed.

"Nu-uh, Bori is a smart girl. She'll get it sooner or later." Nano was pushing down now with all his body.

"Oh, I have no doubt, but you'll get quicker results if you speak dog..." Nano gave her a confused look and laughed.

"Like there's such a thing?" Nano sounded indecisive, because he knew his sister was famous for her tricks.

"Pay attention!"

Nano did.

Téa placed her hand partially opened in front of Bori's nostrils. "Wouf!" she barked. Pressing forward on the dog's nose forced her to walk backwards until the animal ran out of space, having no other choice but to sit. Téa immediately gave her the chunk of bread and praised her with exaggerated jubilee, mostly to conceal the animal's munching. The girl repeated the trick one more time, and Nano couldn't believe his eyes. Bori was now happily wagging her tail and following Téa while poking her nostril at the girl's pocket impatiently.

"Since when do you speak dog?" He believed her. "Can you teach me!?" Nano said excitedly.

"I don't think I can, I'll get in trouble," Téa said.

"Why? Who is going to know? Téa pleeeease!" Nano begged.

"Alright, but pay attention, because this is a task that took me years to master," Téa announced proudly.

"Wow, Téa. I can't believe you know how to do this. How long will it take me to learn? How many dogs did you practice with before you got it?" She didn't expect her little brother to think it through so much, but thankfully Nano was naïve enough not to understand the importance of his questions.

"Eh, it doesn't matter now. Just pay attention." Téa redirected his attention by re-enacting the whole shebang over and over until she ran out of bread. Thankfully, it was getting late. Dark rain clouds had moved in and it had begun to drizzle. Mother was quick to call the two in.

"Time for a bath and dinner," Mother announced.

Mother was surprised to see Téa getting in the water first, which upset Lola very much.

"Get out! Now!" Lola barked.

Téa was going to get out, but mother grabbed Lola by the arm and pulled her close until she could reach her ear. "Let her be...you don't get to see her doing this often..."

"But..." interrupted Lola.

"Just wait to go last and you can change the water...I already have a big pot about to boil." Lola seemed more relaxed after Mother's reassurances.

A basket of soft boiled eggs were waiting at the dinner table with another basket of bread chunks for dipping.

Téa was first to the table and was pleased to see more bread for her tricks. She took a handful and ran to her bedroom to hide it under her mattress. She then went back to her seat and waited for Mother to serve her dinner portion.

With what was supposed to be a "full belly meal," Téa went to bed. Luckily her brother couldn't finish his second egg, so Téa was nice enough to finish it for him.

Both kids jumped on the bed, and Mother came to give her blessings with a kiss to each of their foreheads. "Good night, sleep tight, don't let the bed bugs bite."

"Good night, Mother!" they sang together.

They both giggled and talked in whispers until mother had to knock on their half-opened bedroom door a few times to make them stop. It wasn't until mother threatened them with a good whipping that they chose to switch to the quieter game of, "see who can keep their eyes open the longest." That's all it took for both to fall asleep almost instantly.

Morning came with more drizzling rain and outside looked more like night than day.

Mother stormed into Téa's room with something in her hands and yelled at the two sleeping kids. "Téa, Nano, get up at once!" She rushed to yank open the curtains.

Seeing that the two children seemed to still be sleeping peacefully, she took Nano from under his covers and carried him to her bed. "Téa get up, there are ants all over the place, and for some reason they are all heading to your room!" Téa jumped out of bed with her eyes still closed.

"Must be the rain... these little creatures must know something we don't know, and maybe a stronger storm is heading our way," Mother said.

"Ants? Why?" She had forgotten about the bread she had hidden under her mattress.

Mother began to shake the old rusty can of ant killer dust. "Get out Téa and join your brother in my bed."

It didn't take Mother long to find the cause for the ant infestation. With a handful of bread covered in ants, she left the room, "What is this doing under your mattress?" Téa didn't know what to say.

"What's the matter? Cat got your tongue?" Mother was trying really hard not to laugh.

"You have got to be more careful with that appetite of yours Téa, or you are going to get fat." Téa breathed a sigh of relief.

"Get dressed, we're going to visit Mrs. Milagros." Mother wasn't smiling this time.

"But it's raining!" Téa whined.

"Since when did a little rain stop me from doing my job? Get dressed Téa."

Téa rolled over to hug her brother, but he wasn't there. He never left the bed before her, but when she heard his little voice making barking sounds, she understood.

As she was about to dress, a loud clap of thunder made her jump. The little drizzle had become a heavy shower. Mother came back to her room. "Don't bother getting dressed, no one is going anywhere today." As soon as she left, Téa danced a little happy dance.

So thankful that she didn't have to face Mrs. Milagros, Téa went and hugged her mother, who was making a migote for Nano. "Do you want a migote or toast?" She saw the bread was already broken up and said, "Toast please, and may I have some of these bread chunks?" Mother nodded.

She took a few and went to where her brother was trying to make Bori understand his new found language.

"Here! Give her one of these while pushing her gently, and she'll sit for you." Nano did as he was told. Bori sat for him, and the satisfied master gave her the treat. Joyfully amused, the boy repeated the trick again and again.

## CHAPTER FIFTEEN

## *Never*

When Mother said that no one was going anywhere, she meant it. However, after a couple of days of constant rain, it got to be quite depressing, and even a visit to Mrs. Milagros' seemed like a good idea.

Mother and Téa were at the big iron gate when Mother stopped to fix her daughter's hair by wetting her fingers with a little bit of saliva. "There, much better." Téa was disgusted, but tried not to be too obvious. The house wasn't far, but with the obstacles of rain puddles between the gate and the door, it made it a bit more challenging.

They took off their muddy shoes and left them outside before entering the kitchen, which was located on the back of the house. The cook was busy kneading dough for fresh bread but welcomed them with a nod as she dried her forehead. "Good morning, Tomasina, how is life treating you?" Téa's mother asked politely.

"Ah, it could be worse...I ain't one to complain." The cook stopped to wash her hands.

"I hear you," Mrs. León said as she stooped down on her knees to put a pair of clean house slippers on Téa's feet that she had brought with them in a cloth bag. "How is Mrs. Milagros doing?" she asked before heading to the orchard.

"Mm, she has seen better days, but I think she is feeling a little better today...looks like it is going to be sunny today." Tomasina rang the bell that was intended to call the servants. "By the way, could you pick a few of those tasty plums for me?"

"Don't I always?" Mrs. León shook her head.

"I know, I know..." The maid entered the kitchen before Tomasina could say anything else. They both stared at her.

"You called...why are you both looking so surprised to see me?" She always sounded snobbish around the rest of the help.

"Oh, yes, can you let Mrs. Milagros know Téa is here to visit if she is up to it?"

"Are you kidding me? That's all she's been talking about since she woke up this morning. Follow me, young lady." Téa, standing motionless, looked at her mother who signed for the child to go with the maid.

"I'm glad you're here. Between the rain and Mrs. Milagros, I wanted to shoot myself." Téa giggled. "I'm not being funny." The maid put on her brakes causing Téa to bump into her, which made her laugh even harder.

"Is that you, Téa?" Mrs. Milagros' voice traveled from her room as the maid hushed the girl.

The maid took Téa's hand and pulled her quickly until they reached Mrs. Milagros' door.

"Yes ma'am, here she is." The maid, now in Mrs. Milagros' eye range, acted as if she had never been rude in her life.

"Come!" Téa's fears seemed to dissipate as she walked closer to sit on the rocking chair by Mrs. Milagros' bed.

The old woman patted her bed while giving the maid a look of dismissal.

"Come on silly girl, I'm not contagious, just old," she commented as she noticed Téa's hesitancy.

Téa tried unsuccessfully to climb on the foot of the large bed. The old lady smiled. "Please use the small stool under my bed before you hurt yourself."

Téa got on her knees, and with her arm tried to feel around for it. She felt something and dragged it out, the stench of urine announcing that she had grabbed the wrong thing.

"Be careful not to grab my chamber pot, the maid hasn't had a chance to change it yet." The old lady giggled when she heard Téa huff.

*Now she tells me.*

Téa couldn't hide the look of disgust drawn all over her face. "I see I'm too late," Mrs. Milagros said with an apologetic tone while the girl positioned the right stool in place.

For a brief moment the two stared at one another as if they were looking for changes. "Get closer, oh my have you grown!" Téa smiled at her comment and kept her thoughts to herself.

"Tell me child, what have you gotten yourself into lately?" The old lady asked, sounding more like a child waiting for her nightly story.

*Has my mother been telling her about me again?*

"Your mother told me your uncle surprised you with a puppy."

*I guess she has.* Téa hid her annoyance with a perpetual smile.

"Yep, a surprise that should last me for many birthdays and even a few Christmases as well."

"Wasn't that nice of him." Mrs. Milagros petted the girl on her leg. "You make sure to bring your puppy so we can meet." Téa nodded.

"Her name is Bori!" Téa said.

"That sounds like a boy's name, doesn't it?"

"It was my brother's idea, but I like it."

Mrs. Milagros stared at Téa. "I have a surprise for you too." Mrs. Milagros seemed as if the puppy conversation was not of interest to her.

Téa was afraid to ask, but she did anyway; "So...what is it?"

"I'm not telling you yet." Téa looked unfazed. "I'm waiting for his arrival. He should be here any moment now."

Mrs. Milagros was right, a knock on the door and the voice of her maid announced the surprise "Mrs. Milagros, the photographer is here."

"Well, tell him to set up in the living room." Relieved, Téa was able to breathe realizing it wasn't a trip to who knows where.

As soon as the maid disappeared, Mrs. Milagros turned her head to Téa. "Quick! Open my wardrobe...look for a big box on the bottom end and bring it to me."

The girl did as she was told but was having trouble opening the big antique door. "The lock is broken." She tried again. "It won't open," Téa said as she turned the small iron key.

"I always keep it unlocked, you just locked the door when you tried to open it. Just turn it back where it was."

Téa did, and there it was. She picked up the large box with extreme care, "It's heavy!" Téa said as she gently placing it on the bed.

"Open it."

Téa couldn't believe her eyes, inside the box was the most beautiful dress she have ever seen in her life, made of royal blue velvet with silk lace. Téa was speechless.

"Well, put it on. We don't have all day." Mrs. Milagros had no problem getting up from her bed, and like a proud mother, she helped Téa change into her new gown.

"Mrs. Milagros, I don't know how to thank you."

"Don't, the dress is not yours to keep," the old woman said as she finished with the last button. Téa was speechless again, but this time because a heat of embarrassment rushed through her chest.

*So much for the surprise, a gift I can't keep.*

"Oh! I'm sorry my child; I didn't mean to upset you...of course it's yours, but since you would only wear it on special occasions, like today, it's best to keep it here for safe keeping."

Téa didn't understand why a dress needed to be safe. The girl was disappointed, but she learned a while back that with Mrs. Milagros it was best to agree.

The old lady told Téa to help her with her house coat, which looked more like a fancy silk coat than a housecoat. It had delicate soft thin white feathers adorning the neck. The old woman opened one of her drawers and took out a velvety black box. In it was a long pearl necklace. "A lady is more of a lady with pearls...don't you think Téa?" The girl nodded as Mrs. Milagros dabbed a few drops of perfume on the back of her earlobes with the top cap of a small crystal bottle.

Mrs. Milagros tried to put some on her, but the girl took a few steps back blowing the scent away from her with her hands. "Oh Téa, I keep forgetting you're too young to appreciate these forms of indulgence just yet," Mrs. Milagros said with a smile.

"Ready?" she said placing her wrinkled hand on Téa's shoulder. The girl nodded again.

Téa was in love with how her dress looked, but not with how it felt. It was itchy and *heavy as crap*. Nevertheless the two made it to the living room where the photographer waited with his fake smile.

"Beautiful, just beautiful." The photographer kept on and on praising his targets with his baritone voice that sounded fake as well. He kept reaching for Téa's face and rearranging her chin, then her mouth; he seemed annoyed with the poor little girl.

When the photo session was over, the old fool held Mrs. Milagros hand, and when he tried to kiss it, she removed it with the grace typical of her class.

"How about a nice cup of hot chocolate with churros?" Téa's eyes opened wide.

"But...isn't it time for lunch? Never mind..." Téa quickly said, correcting herself.

"You'd rather have lunch? I'm definitely in the mood for something sweet...after all...no one is going to starve, right?" The old lady smiled at Téa. "I'll be waiting in the tea room."

Téa happily returned her beautiful dress to its box and put it back in the old wardrobe, leaving its door exactly the way it was, unlocked.

In her simpler, but more comfortable attire, she headed toward the sweet smell of chocolate coming from the kitchen. "Where is my mother?" the girl asked loudly, making the cook jump out of her trance. Téa giggled and apologized as she picked up the tray full of steaming churros. "One of these days you're going to kill me!" she exclaimed. "Where are you going with those churros? I'm not done yet." The cook grabbed the tray from Téa and gave it a generous dusting of powdered sugar all over.

"Child, it better be the last time you sneak up on me like that, I'm too old for that shit."

"Sorry..." She apologized again, yet the cook slapped the girl's hand.

"Hey, I said that I was sorry!" Téa cried.

"That one is for trying to steal a churro without my consent."

"Alright, alright, may I have a churro please?" she giggled.

"No, and before I forget, your mother said to stay put, and she'll be back for you later." Tomasina took the tray from Téa and gave it to the angry looking maid who was standing there hand ready and waiting.

"You need to stop wandering around. Mrs. Milagros has been asking for you." The maid took the tray and pushed Téa in front of her to make sure she didn't vanish again.

"There she is!" Mrs. Milagros said with excitement.

The chocolate was waiting on the table in a shiny metal jug with a saucer covering the open top to keep the heat from escaping.

The two sat side by side, and like two little girls, dunked churros over and over into their wide china cups. "Look at you Téa, you have chocolate drizzle all over your mouth. Let me fix it..." She took her churro, which was saturated with dark chocolate, and poked the girl's face with it, "for the picture." Téa was surprised by her silliness. Mrs. Milagros chuckled like never before. Téa reacted with the same maneuver, but Mrs. Milagros was ready and saw her coming. The girl ended up with more chocolate stains, this time on her dress. Téa nervously laughed. She couldn't believe the old lady was behaving more like her. The maid arrived with a jug of fresh water. Her professional stone face didn't let her inner disapproval show, but her knuckles turned white as she held the water pitcher. It was a big chocolate mess.

"Calm down now, you hear? I'm thirsty," Mrs. Milagros said as she wiped Téa's face clean.

"Now, Téa, do you remember the conversation we had about school?" Téa's face turned sour.

"That's not funny Mrs. Milagros. I told you I don't want your money, and I don't want to leave my family...especially my little brother, for school" She was thinking about Bori too.

"Alright, alright. No need to get this way..." she said backing off in fear that she would lose Téa again.

"Well, at least come see me like you used to child...you bring me life..." Her eyes started to gloss over with tears.

Téa sighed, "I will, but please...no more school talk, ok?"

Mrs. Milagros dabbed at her tears with a white napkin. "Alright, I promise to never again bring up school or the nuns."

"Never, never?" Téa wanted reassurances.

"Never, never!" Mrs. Milagros cried as she held onto the little girl's hands.

"It's getting late," Téa said, seeing that her mother wasn't coming. "I got to go," she said bluntly. The old lady loved her little friend's disposition to speak her mind, so she let her go.

Téa wasn't surprise that her busy mother wasn't there to pick her up since their house wasn't that far.

Closer to home, Téa was pleased to see her brother playing with Bori, but more so just to smell the air coming from her home. For once she was tired of sweets, and for once she wanted real food.

Boris joyfully ran to greet her as soon as she heard her whistle. The girl squatted down and waited with her arms wide open and her eyes closed for her furry friend to knock her to the ground and lick her face.

"My, my, Bori, calm down girl! It's not like I was gone for a year." Téa walked the remaining distance with Bori jumping up and down and from side to side.

"Hey Nano." Téa was hungry but made time for her little brother.

"Hey," he answered unenthusiastically.

"Are you okay?" Téa sat by him under the two giant mulberry trees that gave them gifts of good shade, fresh leaves for Nano's collection of silkworms, and of course all of the yummy mulberries their stomachs could carry.

"These bread chunks only work when you are not here." Téa looked at his little hand, took one and ate it.

"Mmm...not bad, but who can resist a shirt with all these chocolate stains? Not any dog in their right mind," Téa chuckled while stretching her shirt so Bori could get to the stains.

"Oh, that explains it...it's all about the yumminess." Nano seemed content.

Téa was happy to kill two birds with one stone. Her brother was happy that the dog would go with who ever had the tastiest treat, and mother wasn't going to have to scrub too hard to remove the stains.

Mother hollered the magic words, "Supper is ready!" The two siblings didn't hesitate.

"Yum, yum, the food has been smelling like it's ready for hours!" Nano said while licking his lips.

"You always say that..." Mother sang. "As soon as I throw the chopped onions in the hot grease."

"Mmm...Artichoke and peas stew! My favorite!" Téa added.

"Téa do you want your egg fried or poached?" Mother asked as Téa and her brother responded "fried!" in unison. She asked the same question every time, and every time she got the same answer. Heaven forbid the one time she assumed what they would want... that would be the time they would change their mind.

The brother's weren't back from the fields, and father was still asleep, so it was just the three of them dunking their bread in the delicious broth and in the milky film covering the soft, bright orange egg yolk. No one spoke but the munching sounds said it all. Bori combed the floor under the big dining table for the small treats that her three favorite people snuck down to her.

"Where is your sister?"

Téa had to break her synchronized dunking to answer. "She left this morning and said she'd be back. I haven't heard from her since."

Mother looked concerned.

"Who wants a slice of the sweetest honeydew melon ever?" announced Lola who burst through the front door with Emilio in tow. He was carrying the big melon for her.

"So that's where she went," Téa whispered to Nano.

"What?" Nano yelled.

"Never mind..." Nano gave her a confused look, as did her mother.

"Sit while I prepare you both a plate?" Mother got up to take the fat melon from Emilio but gave it back as soon as she realized how heavy it was "Here, take it to the kitchen."

"Mother we're not hungry..."

"What do you mean, you're not hungry?" Mother said with knife in hand as she poked the tasty melon.

"Emilio's mother invited me to their table and I didn't want to be rude." Lola held out a large plate for the melon.

"Of course you didn't want to be rude..." Mother hated it when she didn't know her children's whereabouts, no matter how old they were. "Oh, what the heck, that leaves more for your brothers; they can sure put away some food...just one thing, don't leave without telling us again. Do you hear?" Lola gave her an apologetic nod.

"Mother, I can smell that honeydew all the way from here," Téa hollered.

"Lolilla," that's what Mother would call her daughter when in a good mood. "Do you care for a piece or have you had some already?" Even though she was a country woman, Mrs. León was soft spoken and sensitive, something her future son-in-law lacked on many levels. She still couldn't understand what drove her daughter to fall in love with such a brute.

"Oh no, I'm full up to here..." Emilio answered while patting his chest as if Mrs. León were talking to him, then he let out a loud burp. Lola shook her head and so did Mother.

## CHAPTER SIXTEEN

# The Birds and the Bees

"What?" Téa's friendly snap was in response to Mrs. Milagros' stare.

Téa was busy sharing her pastry with some of the little birds that flocked around the fruit trees.

She had won her battle with Mrs. Milagros regarding studying. The old lady felt there was no use in wasting the little time that she had left training the little hellion. She couldn't help but to love the child, and in her mind having her close was more important for now. Mrs. Milagros learned a long time ago to pick her battles, and this one was better left to an old friend, time. Téa would learn her own lessons in time.

"I was wondering...never mind." Mrs. Milagros grabbed the hidden napkin she always carried in her wrist and wiped her tears.

"Mrs. Milagros...why are old people always so teary?" Téa asked with her usual boldness.

The old lady shifted her eyes to the busy little birds bouncing from side to side in search of scraps. "We just are...I guess."

"But this time you're really crying," Téa said.

"No, I just get a little emotional every time I think about certain things."

"What things?" Téa was curious.

"Ah, things that happened a long time ago."

"What?" Téa said, not realizing how insolent she sounded.

"You're too young to understand," the old woman said.

"Try me!"

Mrs. Milagros shook her head in disbelief, "All right, but what I'm about to tell you must stay with you." The old lady had Téa's chin in a clamp.

"Everything is a lie...especially my so called family." She paused a moment to stare at the birds. "You see, my nieces and nephews are like these birds."

"Cute and nice?" Téa asked as she rubbed her chin.

"Only if they want something from me. Like these birds, they would dance around deceivingly. Behind my back they're more like greedy vultures waiting for me..." Mrs. Milagros stopped mid-sentence.

"Waiting for what, Mrs. Milagros?" Téa asked but the old lady ignored her. "Waiting for you to die?"

"You're a smart little one, you know?" Mrs. Milagros wasn't surprised.

"But, you never give them anything and still they come back to see you. They seem nice. They smile at me...sometimes."

"Ha, nice...what they really are is a bunch of hyenas waiting for me to kick the bucket," Mrs. Milagros said as she tossed her handkerchief at the little birds. "You are the only one who comes of your own free will."

"Well..." Téa pulled her shoulders up. "My mother kind of makes me..." Mrs. Milagros froze at the girl's unexpected statement and chuckled.

"See, that's what I love about you...your honesty, I always know where I stand with you." Mrs. Milagros held Téa's hand and said, "Education is an important tool if you don't want to be an easy target.

But you're too young to understand. I just hope that you come to your senses before I die."

"I see the headaches your money gives you. I want none of that," Téa said.

"Little Téa, remember when I told you about my first love?" The girl nodded.

"I merely scratched the surface of my story." Mrs. Milagros lowered her voice and Téa scooted her chair closer.

"I was very much in love, but too young to understand the matters of the heart and its consequences." Téa looked confused but didn't make a sound.

"I was strong as an ox, so I didn't understand why my mother got so nervous when she saw me getting sick in the morning. I guess like any other mother she was worried about why I was so ill. I, on the other hand, naively thought something I ate had caused my morning distress. But I thought it strange that I would bounce back and be perfectly fine until the next morning. It only happened for a few weeks and then it stopped. My health was again impeccable, but then Mother noticed that my breasts began to grow, and I was confused. I didn't know why, but in tears she told me that the stork was going to visit me sometime that same year, and that she had to send me away."

"What's the big deal? I see storks visiting the town's tower and no one goes anywhere," Téa interrupted.

"It means that I was with child; that's what it means. The next thing I knew, my mother sent me away before my belly started to show. She sent me away accompanied by my mother's most trusted confidant to our summer house in Algeciras. No one suspected a thing because I had been attending a school for ladies of high society in France. I was sad, but she didn't care. She just wanted me away from that *despicable boy*, as she called him. I had disgraced my family by getting pregnant out of wedlock, and worse still, with a common gardener."

"What happened to the baby?" Téa sounded sad.

"Just when I thought my mother's intentions were to keep me there until I delivered the baby, I soon discovered that wasn't the case. The daughter of our summer house keeper; who after many summers had become my friend, told me what she had overheard my guardian tell her mother in confidence..." Mrs. Milagros took a sip from her drink and stared at her glass in silence. Téa took a gulp of water while she waited for her to recuperate.

"Well, I don't know if I should. Has anyone explained anything to you?"

"Anything about what?"

"Well, about the birds and the bees?" Téa was looking at the birds as if they would give her a hint.

"See, you are too innocent to hear something like this." The old lady was determined.

"What? But, I'm not, I swear..." Téa wasn't happy.

"See? That's what I'm talking about. You need not only an education but a good shot of manners as well my child." Mrs. Milagros seemed so sad. "Either way, it's getting late."

Téa took Mrs. Milagros' hand and kissed her.

"Tomorrow I'll be back with my books, and I will make you proud."

The girl took off and yelled from the gate, "But don't get any ideas, I'll go to hell before I go to those nuns!" Mrs. Milagros shook her head, but she was pleased; she had hope.

On her way home, Téa couldn't stop thinking about the birds and especially the bees. *Did the birds eat the bees? Or no wait...maybe the bees stung the birds...*

She wanted to know about it so badly but knew she couldn't ask her mother.

Upon her arrival, the house was clean and tidy. The only sound was coming from the kitchen. It was the sound of water being splashed and the clinking of plates.

"Hello!" Téa yelled.

"It's about time you got home, you lazy little shit!" snapped Lola, who always complained of having to do all the house chores by herself.

Téa would normally turn around and run rather than put up with her sister's bullying but Lola was her only option if she wanted to find out about '*the birds and the bees.*'

"Sorry, but you know I can't leave Mrs. Milagros until she tells me I can," Téa said.

"Yes, yes, excuses and more excuses ... come and help me dry these plates."

Lola pushed a large white cloth against Téa's chest. "Here, start drying the plates for me."

Téa took one, wiped the front, then the back, and then placed it on the table where two other dry plates awaited. The small table was next to a cabinet that her brother Antonio built into an opening in the wall. It was covered by a curtain made of simple cloth.

"Lola?" Téa wanted to ask the question, but was afraid of her sister's reaction.

"Yes?" Téa had been drying the same plate front and back for a little too long.

"Téa you're supposed to dry them, not shine them. What is it?" Lola snapped the plate out of her sister's hands.

"Well..."

"Well, what? Come on, I don't have all day."

"What do you know about the birds and the bees?"

Surprised, Lola's eyes grew large and began to cough nervously. She had choked on her own saliva as she was swallowing. She never expected that kind of question from her little sister, not in a million years...or at least not yet.

"Are you choking?" Téa said, patting her sister's back.

Lola shook her head, "It's just my saliva went down the wrong tube," she said between coughs.

As soon as Lola recovered from the shock, she answered, "You need to stop eavesdropping on women talking. It's none of your business. You'll have time to learn about the damn birds and the bees soon enough."

Lola took another wet plate and shoved it into Téa's chest. "Here, do the same to this one."

"I knew you couldn't help me; you probably don't know either." Téa was trying to trick her sister into telling her.

"Of course I know, Fluffy!" Lola had begun calling her little sister *Fluffy* when her hair began to grow back.

"Don't call me that! You..."

"You, what?" Lola knew what her little sister was about to call her, since she had gained weight and was now a bit on the heavy side.

"You keep eating the way you are, and I'll be calling you "Fat Fluffy!" Lola shot back.

"Now that...that was uncalled for! Take-it-back." Téa said.

"Or what?" Lola threw her arm out and broke the porcelain plate in half that Téa had been holding.

Téa had never seen her sister react that way. "Oh my God!" Téa exclaimed when she saw her sister's arm bleeding.

"What?" Lola said nonchalantly, "It didn't hurt." But when she felt a tickle running down her arm and looked to investigate, the older sister fell to the floor at the sight of a deep cut.

Téa didn't hesitate. She took the white cloth for drying plates and wrapped it around her sister's wound.

"Lola I'm sorry, please say something!" Téa cried.

Lola didn't move. "Lola please wake up...I didn't mean it!" Téa was now on top of her.

"Get off!" Lola pushed her off. "Go look for mother!" Téa didn't move, "Go I said!"

Téa left and quickly found her mother, who instructed her to find the doctor. She had never run so fast in her life. "Quick Doctor, my sister is dying!" Téa yelled as soon as the man opened his door.

He tried unsuccessfully to keep up with Téa; thankfully he had been there many times before.

Once he arrived, everyone felt better. "This is nothing a few stiches can't fix," the good doctor said while preparing the bandage.

"Now you two need to make amends and act more your age. Especially you, Lola." their mother said.

"It was all an accident," Lola complained while she looked at the doctor's work of art.

"How does it feel? Is it too tight?" the doctor asked Lola before he finished the wrapping.

"Nope, it's just right," Lola sang.

"Thank you, doctor, for coming so fast," Mrs. León said as she handed the man a paper bag full of brown eggs and a bottle of fresh milk.

"Oh, it was nothing." He looked at his payment, took it and left.

Mother turned around as soon as the doctor was far enough away, "So, what was all this about?"

Téa looked at her big sister who answered, "Nothing Mother, just like I said before...it was all an accident. Téa was helping me with the plates. I shook my arm trying to scare a fly away and bumped her plate, breaking it. That's all," Lola said.

The cut was in the lower arm, and the doctor had ordered a few days of rest so that it could heal properly. That meant Téa had to do all of her sister's work.

The few days didn't go by quickly, for either of them, but Téa took the opportunity to ask her sister about the forbidden subject every chance she got. Lola was not good at being patient, seeing as Téa was very good at making a nuisance of herself. But, Lola stood her ground and didn't tell her a thing.

CHAPTER SEVENTEEN

# Red and Blue

"Téa, let's go!" Mother yelled, then mumbled, "What could possibly be taking her so long? TÉA!" Still no answer.

"Téa, we need to get going!" she yelled as she entered her daughter's room.

"I'm here, mother..." Mother looked all over the room but still couldn't see her. "Down here..." Her daughter's voice echoed from under the bed.

"Child? What have you lost there?" Mrs. León said, now on her knees peeking into darkness under the bed.

"I can't find it."

"You can't find what?"

"The notebook Mrs. Milagros gave me." Téa coughed as she vigorously moved the boxes stored under the bed from side to side frantically searching for her notebook.

"Who knows? I don't even remember seeing you with it. Come out from under there before the dust kills you."

"Mother, I promised her I would bring my notebook!" she cried as her mother tried to pull her into the middle of the room.

"Well, I'm sure you're not going to shock her. Just tell her you lost it."

"But, that's just it. I didn't lose it! I'm positive that's where I kept the thing, in one of these boxes. Someone took it!" Téa insisted.

"And who may I ask would borrow your notebook, and I say borrowed because we have no thieves in this family. Besides, it is not like any of us would be excited to see a notebook! Your brothers are too busy with work, and I can hardly sign my name... No one took your book." She pulled harder this time.

Téa quit her whining and decided to do as her mother had suggested.

On their way to Mrs. Milagros' house, Téa finally found the courage to ask her mother about the question that had been bothering her for nearly three weeks. "Mother, Mrs. Milagros mentioned something about *the birds and the bees,* but she wasn't sure you would approve..." Téa hesitated. "I asked Lola about it, and she said it was none of my damn business."

"I don't know why she wouldn't want you to know about the birds and the bees. It's pretty simple. The birds lay eggs just as a woman carries a baby in her womb, and men carry the pollen when going from flower to flower, just like a bee."

That explanation didn't help, and Téa was now more confused than ever.

"Tell you what, I'll let Mrs. Milagros explain it to you. With her good education, I'm sure she'll be able to clear up the whole thing." Téa gave her mother a satisfied nod.

As mother and daughter neared the house, the cook was standing in the kitchen door about to throw out the hot water she had used to boil cabbage.

"Good day Tomasina, having stomach problems again?" Téa's mother laughed.

"Ha, very funny. This woman and her belief that cabbage is good for you," Tomasina said as she avoided the putrid steam. "Losing weight, that's all it's good for."

"Well, maybe that's not such a bad thing," Mrs. León said looking at the cook's voluptuous figure.

"Ha, ha, very funny. I don't want to lose weight. My husband loves my curves," she said while patting her love handles.

They both chuckled.

"Mrs. Milagros is in the garden with her roses."

Mrs. León turned around and bumped into Téa who quickly stepped out of her way then followed her obediently. As they drew closer, Mrs. Milagros' twig of a silhouette became more visible. She was too busy trimming the leaves of her beautiful roses to notice anything else.

"Hello!" Téa ran the last few feet, making the old lady miss the leaf and cut a rose from its stem instead.

"Look what you made me do."

"Sorry," Téa apologized as she picked up the decapitated rose from the ground. She really meant it.

Mrs. León also apologized for her daughter, "I'm so sorry Mrs. Milagros, my stupid daughter..."

"It's alright, it was an accident." She took the rose from Téa's hand and stuck the stem in her hair bun. "There, see?"

Mrs. Milagros looked at Mrs. León, "Thank you for bringing me back my Téa."

Mrs. León pleasantly shook her head and left. She went home with an uneasy feeling remembering how the lady referred to Téa as hers.

"Where is your notebook, forgotten at home?"

"I know you must think that I'm not serious because I didn't bring my notebook, but I couldn't find it...it was not where I left it." Mrs. Milagros wasn't concerned.

Changing the subject, she handed an extra pair of trimmers to Téa saying, "Help me with these roses, would you? Here, put on these gloves before you start. I don't want you to trim your fingers. You can't be too careful with these things."

"Pay attention to how I do it first, then try," instructed Mrs. Milagros.

Téa began to trim dry leaves without looking at Mrs. Milagros even once.

"Well, well...have you done this before?"

"Many times. Have you forgotten who my parents are?" Téa said. "I'm a country girl."

"My mother said it is okay for the señora to explain all about the birds and the bees...and tell me about the rest of the story. My mother tried, but I don't know..." Téa sighed without taking her eyes off of the roses.

"Really? You don't mind if I check with her first?" Téa shook her head.

"No, I don't mind," she said nonchalantly.

Mrs. Milagros knew she was telling the truth, because Téa didn't hesitate or seem nervous.

"Ah, I believe you." She paused to think.

"My, my...I don't even know where to start."

"How about from the beginning?" Téa said.

"How old are you?" the old lady asked. "Because you truly don't act your age."

"Sorry," Téa complained. "But, are you going to tell me about that night? Yes or no?"

Mrs. Milagros was too tired for a confrontation, so with a sigh she said, "I don't even remember where I left of..."

"I do! It was when your friend told you that horrific story about overhearing her mother and your guardian; you know, the one who became your friend," Téa said without taking a moment to breath.

"I'm impressed you remembered, but then again your mind is so young compared to mine. I can hardly remember my name sometimes."

"Really? I have an uncle that has the same problem. He can't even remember his own family." Mrs. Milagros was exaggerating when she said she couldn't remember her name but felt sorry for Téa's uncle.

"You better tell me that story before you forget!" Téa exclaimed.

"Téa, you're something else, do you know that?" The old lady rubbed the girl's head and Téa shrugged her shoulders.

"My mother knew I was pregnant before I even suspected anything. All I know is that on one of the many afternoons that he spent following us, my mother fell asleep while she read to me. That's when I took the opportunity to go where he was waiting for me. Behind the bushes, we held hands and then kissed. What I thought was supposed to be embarrassing, came as natural as breathing." Mrs. Milagros blushed. "And that's when the birds and the bees came into place."

"Alright?" Téa wanted to know more.

"The bird's egg is the woman's womb and the bees are the ones carrying the seeds in their little feet."

"And what does that have to do with men...?" Téa was so very confused.

"Ah...never mind..." the old lady said. "Just let me get on with the story before I forget where I was." Téa nodded.

"My friend told me what she had overheard. The plan was to wait there until my pregnancy ran its course, and as soon as I had the baby..." The old lady paused, then swallowed.

"Did they give it to another family?" Téa interrupted.

"No child..." Mrs. Milagros' voice sounded troubled. She softly stroked the girl's hair and then continued with her story. "As soon as I gave birth to my baby, their plan was to take it away from me, and then come back to tell me that it was born dead."

"So, what did they do with the baby?" Téa asked.

"Nothing. My friend gave me a potion that was supposed to make me go into labor early..."

"What was it?" Téa was so intrigued.

"I don't know, it was a mix of herbs, cinnamon and warm milk."

"Did it work?" she interrupted the old lady again.

"Not that first night, but the second day my friend gave me more after our daily walk, and that one did it. It was a rainy night. I don't know if it was because I was so afraid of thunder, or if it was everything at once. But, that very night, I went into labor. The pain was unbearable...thank God for the thunder, or my cries would have alerted everyone, and my baby would have been in the wrong hands.

"So, I take it you had your baby...what happened next? Was it a girl or a boy?"

"A girl, a beautiful little girl."

"So what happened?"

"When my friend and I went on our long walks, she had shown me a convent on the outskirts of town. The convent church had a drop box where people used to make donations. However, with times being so hard, all anyone dropped off was a baby. That's how the old convent became an orphanage."

"Is that where you took your baby?"

Mrs. Milagros was too choked up to speak, so with tears in her eyes she just nodded. "I left a note in the basket. I wanted to give her a name, so that when I was able to go looking for her, I would have a head start. She was to be named Vicenta de Paul after the orphanage named for San Vicente de Paul."

"Clever. I take it you never found her," Téa said.

"I never went looking for her," Mrs. Milagros looked away, unbearable shame running through her veins, "My parents had arranged a marriage for me, and that was that. I couldn't look for her, because I was a married woman. I figured I could have more children, and this way, it would make it possible for another couple to adopt her. But God punished me. As you can see, I was never again blessed with a child." She sighed. "So, now you know." Téa took Mrs. Milagros' hand and simply held it.

"I'm sorry."

"Now, this is our secret, you hear me Téa!" The old lady was holding her hand tightly.

"Yes, yes I know, I know how to keep a secret, so you can let go of my hand. You're hurting me." Mrs. Milagros looked as if she were in a trance until Téa broke loose from her clamped grip, making the old lady snap out of her trance.

"I'm sorry my dear, did I hurt you?" The girl's hand was red.

"I'm okay," Téa said as she rubbed her hand.

"We should go to church, you and I," Mrs. Milagros said in an attempt to change the subject.

"Uh, last time I remember going to church was at my first communion, and since then I haven't placed a foot anywhere near... and considering that I haven't lost anything there, why go," Téa said.

"What's the matter? You don't like it? Téa, you need to give it a try...it's quite..."

"What? Fun...? I must say; it's the most boring thing I have ever tried in my life. Nothing tops it. In my mind it takes first place, even before a funeral wake. At least there you can see a dead person, and the drama is quite comical sometimes. In church you can't even fart..."

Mrs. Milagros' mouth gaped open at Téa's comment.

"You know, it echoes!" Téa laughed. "It just gets worse from there! Try taking a nap...it's impossible...with all the up and down, kneel, repeat. Just when you get seated and feel most comfortable, he commands you to stand again. Damn it, it almost looks like the priest enjoys making the old ladies dance." Mrs. Milagros just stared.

"Ok, then, I guess that settles it..." Mrs. Milagros grabbed the sheers with her bare hands and reached for the stem of a rose that was a little too far away.

"Ouch!" She quickly snatched back her hand and pressed her injured finger. She was bleeding quite profusely.

Téa felt nauseated by the sight of so much blood. The lady's veins were so protuberant that you could see shades of blue flowing under her dry paper looking skin.

Téa had overheard her mother talking about Mrs. Milagros' long dynasty of high lineage, blue blood her mother would proudly announce.

Now she had proof for the next time she argued with her mother. She now knew the truth. She bled red just like everyone else.

CHAPTER EIGHTEEN

# The Rabbit Hole

Téa liked to recreate Mrs. Milagros' story in her mind. She thought of the different scenarios that could have taken place if she had been in the same situation. She tried hard to imagine leaving her little brother behind, or even Bori. Téa was sure about one thing; she would never abandoned her baby. Not in a million years.

The girl was faithful to her promise and visited the old lady on a regular basis, not because her mother made her, but because she wanted to.

During the summer, Mrs. Milagros was usually busy entertaining friends, and a few of her scattered family members, most of whom were not wealthy, but pretended to be. Snobs at their best. What they lacked in money, they made up for in stupidity.

All the entertaining meant that Mrs. León was busier than usual, therefore Téa had unsupervised time to roam about. Mother left Lola in charge, but she quickly became lazy and bossy. Especially around her fiancée, to whom she wanted to show off her motherly skills. Téa would have none of that. As soon as Lola started bossing them around, she took Nano and their faithful dog Bori and disappeared. Far enough away to be out of her cross hairs.

It was hot, but they knew better than to go to the beach. There were too many tourists. Mother feared them even more than the ocean's currents. *There are too many weirdos in the crowds. If you could only recognize them, but you can't. Unfortunately, it only takes an instant to snap up a child,* their mother would lecture them every time new people came to town.

"I'm bored!" Nano exclaimed as he lay on the branch of a fig tree chewing on a weed stem.

"No kidding. Now, don't get any ideas about picking up lizards just to amuse yourself," Téa said looking up at her brother from the ground where she sat. Bori, who was tied to a low branch, had dug a shallow hole and lay there quite comfortably; her eyes closed but flickering every once in a while.

"Oh, have no fear Sis." He took a green leaf and used it as a fan.

"You better not, because if you do it again, I might not be so lucky and could really die. For real." Téa copied her brother and made a fan out of a leaf to chase away the heat.

"Téa let's go to the cemetery." Téa wasn't afraid of one dead person, but she was terrified to have so many in one place. All those crosses, vaults and pantheons. She had watched too many scary movies.

"Let's not and say we did," Téa responded.

"But Sis, it's so cool there," Nano replied as he jumped down from his tree branch.

"How many times do I have to tell you that you shouldn't go there by yourself?"

"Why? There're only dead people, and they can't hurt you. They are DEAD, you know!" Nano giggled when she stood up and began to chase after him. Téa followed her little brother to the cemetery, begging him between nervous laughs to stop running. Bori, who had been left behind, pulled on her rope and barked.

"Stop running, Nano, pleeese, I promise I won't hurt you!" she yelled. "Much...little shit," she mumbled.

Téa couldn't believe how fast her little brother had become. She watched him from afar as he entered the ghostly white entrance to the graveyard, without hesitation, and with no fear.

Téa was frightened, and it was very clear to her that she was not crossing through the gate entrance. She always declined her mother's invitation to accompany her while paying her respects to the dead. Téa would argue, "I have all eternity to spend in that place... and I would rather wait until after I am dead to start."

She stopped at the entrance and looked around. "Nano?" She was afraid her little brother would try to scare her if she entered. She just stood there.

The large entrance was an arch composed of two black iron doors that were kept open granting access during the day, but closed at night. Rocking in the *Levante* winds stood enormous cypress trees which had grown higher than the walls surrounding the cemetery. The immaculately white-washed walls, which were four meters high and built of stucco, stood side by side with the large skinny trees. Téa's arms were covered with goose bumps at the sound of the ghostly howls the green giants seemed to mimic as they danced with the wind.

Téa yelled once more for her brother, but only her echo answered. With no sign of Nano, she was gradually becoming concerned. Suddenly a bird fell from the sky and landed at her feet. The tomboy jumped and screamed like a girl. She was terrified. The poor creature was not dead, but was bleeding.

"Nano, what the hell! You better come out, because I'm not going in!" she yelled.

"I'm leaving!" she sang.

"Nano, I swear to God; I'm not kidding!" Téa was making the sign of the cross with her foot in the loose sand.

"Fine, suit yourself!" Téa waited a little then ran back to their house.

Frantically, she searched for Lola who was nowhere to be found. The house was empty.

She ran out of the house desperate to find anyone, this time calling for her mother.

Téa was relieved when she saw her sister coming out of the chicken pen "Nano is gone!" Téa yelled.

"What! He's gone? Where?" Lola was combing her hair with her hands.

"What were you doing in the chicken pen?" Téa couldn't help but think of the birds and the bees.

"Nothing, just getting some eggs," Lola said nonchalantly, as she brushed her skirt down.

*Where are they then...* Téa suspected Emilio was not far away.

"Quick you've got to help me, Nano is in the graveyard, and he refuses to come out!" Téa pulled on her sister's dress in an attempt to rush her.

"Wait a minute, he's gone there many times. He'll come home when he's ready."

"But..." Téa said.

"But nothing," Lola jerked her dress back from her sister's hand.

"Mmmm sister...where are the eggs?" Lola looked at her hands as if she were surprised the eggs weren't there.

"Never mind the eggs. Téa you might be right... let's go check on Nano. Lord knows mother would kill us if something happened to him."

On the way back to the cemetery, Téa told her sister about the incident with the bird. Lola was too upset to even care. All she could think about was her boyfriend left alone in the chicken pen.

"Lola, aren't you scared to go in by yourself?"

Lola gave her a goofy look, "By myself? You're coming in with me roly-poly." Lola had given her that nickname when she first found Téa all rolled up under the sheets when she was afraid.

"Naha...no way!"' Téa cried.

"Come on, nothing can hurt you as long as you keep yourself near me. No one messes with Lola," she chuckled.

"What about the dead bird?"

"I'm sure there's a reasonable explanation behind it." Lola said firmly. She dragged Téa toward the cemetery.

"What's that noise?" Téa made her sister stop.

"It's us!" Lola jerked her straight. "Roly-poly relax," Lola said with a smile.

As they walked, Lola called her brother's name over and over, but still no answer. Téa echoed her sister's call, each time with more confidence.

"Silly me..., scared...scared of what?" At that exact moment a ghostly looking shape jumped from behind a tree.

Téa ran away like a bat out of hell, screaming obscenities.

"What the hell?" Lola screamed and instantly began to slap the unknown thing.

"Stop, stop, ouch! That hurts!" one of the Varea brothers cried as the white sheet came off revealing his sweaty red face.

"You scared my little sister, you idiot!" Lola said. "Look what you did, I had her convinced there is no such thing as a ghost." Lola was livid.

"Yep! I think she peed her pants." The other brother chuckled as he came out of his hiding place. The ghost laughed too, but was soon silenced by the slap of Lola's hand on the side his head. She slapped him so hard his sling shot dropped from his back pocket.

"What the hell are you guys doing here?" Lola asked.

"Playing," they both answered at once.

"Playing in a sacred place? You should be ashamed." The brothers shrugged their shoulders.

"I should tell my father." They both shook their head with fear.

Nano comes here too! Look, he's over there asleep..." They pointed to an empty niche.

"Where?" Lola asked.

Nano was sleeping in what would one day, hold a coffin. He looked dead.

"What the hell are you doing in this thing?" She yanked him out.

"Ouch! Ouuuch! Let go!" Nano cried.

"You have some explaining to do. You are in so much trouble!" Lola carried him on her back. "Aren't you grossed out to crawl inside those things? They're full of webs and bugs."

"I don't care. The bugs are my friends, and it feels so cool in there. You should try it Sis," Nano sincerely recommended.

"Not in a million years!" Lola's body shook with disgust.

"Nano, you shouldn't hang out with those two; they are too old for you. Did you know they shot a bird today?" Lola said.

"Na uh!"

"Yep, they each had a sling shot in their back pocket," Lola accused.

"Only for target practice! Look, I have one too!" Nano showed his to Lola.

"Umm, what target?" Lola asked as she sat the boy on the ground.

"A bunch of rusted cans, that's all. Never birds." Lola knew he was telling the truth.

"Maybe they practiced on them while you were busy playing dead?" Lola looked up into his little glossy eyes while tying his shoelaces.

"How did you know I was playing dead?" Nano asked.

"I don't know! Maybe because you're you. You need to take a break from those mummy films and that Boris Kar... or whatever his name is..."

"Boris...Boris Karloff!" Nano assured his sister.

"Okay, enough of him. Let's hope Mother isn't home yet." Lola began to walk faster.

Happy to find the house still empty, neither their mother nor their brothers were home yet, and Father was at his usual afternoon game of dominos at the local tavern.

"Where is everyone?" Father's voice echoed on Lola's back.

"In the fields, you know that Father." Lola turned around, startled to find her father at home.

"And your mother? Where is your mother?" he asked as he headed in the direction of his room.

"Working at Mrs. Milagros'..."

"I'm tired...I'm taking a nap...wake me up when your mother gets here," Father said.

"Yes, Father. Okay Nano, you too. Go take a nap while I look for Téa."

As she walked towards the chicken pen, Lola stared at the little shed with nostalgia. A cry broke the spell.

Lola ran in the direction she was certain it had come from. "What's wrong!" she yelled.

"It's Bori, she's trapped!" Téa was on her knees and digging frantically at a rabbit hole.

"How?" Lola couldn't see the dog, no matter how hard she looked.

"I was playing catch with her. My stick spooked a small rabbit, and she chased after it instead! Please Sister, get her out!" Téa begged.

"How?" Lola began to help her sister dig.

They kept digging, but the wall was crumbling, causing the entry to completely collapse.

"LOLA, she's going to die if we don't get her out!" Téa screamed as she heard Bori's cries.

Lola got up and ran.

"Where're you going? Don't leave me!" Téa yelled.

"I'll be right back...we need help!"

Lola screamed for her father all the way home.

"Father, Father, wake up!" Lola shook him.

"What? What! Damn it, already," her father mumbled.

"Father come quickly! Téa needs help!"

Antonio jumped up, thankful his shoes were still on his feet.

When her father saw Téa on the ground, he fell to her side. "TÉA!" he screamed as he swept her up.

"Father, its Bori!" Téa cried. "She's trapped!"

"We'll get her out!" Father exclaimed. "We need a shovel."

He remembered the one in the chicken pen.

"Lola there's one in the chicken pen, go get it."

He began to dig while Téa ran for the shovel, and Lola stood there like a mummy.

Téa was back, and Lola was still unable to react. Téa cried for Bori.

"Father you're hurting her!"

He continued to dig intensely, ignoring his daughter's pleas.

"Lola, take your sister home!" Father ordered.

"No, Bori needs me!"

"Téa, she is going to die, and I don't want you to see that!" Father yelled.

Lola pulled her sister's arm, but Téa seemed to be glued to the ground.

"Father!" his son Diego yelled from afar. Faster than the wind, he was there to help.

"There's nothing you can do son. She's probably dead by now," Father said sadly as he dropped the shovel and began to walk home.

Diego looked at Téa, who was digging at the ground with her small hands. "Bori, please don't die, hang in there! Pleeeease baby girl, I know you're strong!" Téa collapsed. Diego had never seen his sister cry that hard.

Téa sobbed, begging God to save her dog. Suddenly the ground began to shift. It looked like Bori was a fighter after all.

Diego began digging with even more energy than before. Even though he had been working in the fields all day, he dug and dug, charging into the sand with extreme force. He thrust the shovel again and must have hit something, and it must have been Bori, because the animal started to scream so loud that you would have thought all hell had broken loose.

Lola, Téa and Diego dug with their hands until they freed Bori's head. The rest of her languid body was then quickly pulled free as well. They carefully dusted her body, which was encrusted with moist dirt. Her eyes were covered too. She held her mouth open and her tongue, also full of dirt, leaned out and to one side. The poor animal began to cough mucus mixed with wet sand. She was having difficulty breathing, and Diego started mouth to mouth. Téa cried while Lola held her. Just when Diego thought the battle was lost, the animal responded with a big jerk. He patted her softly when he realized Bori had a good reason for screaming; her leg had a big gap, and it was bleeding profusely.

Diego took his shirt off and wrapped it around the wounded limb. He carried her home with Téa rubbing her head the whole way.

"Bori, you are going to be alright," Téa whispered in tears.

"Yes, she will," Diego said.

He gave Lola a sad look, and his sister shook her head softly.

CHAPTER NINETEEN

T éa's feelings of guilt grew as Bori's ability to run was diminished by a noticeable limp. She was now tied to a tree or kept on a leash.

"Téa, you have to keep her on a leash if you want her to go with you," Mother instructed. "I know it's not the same, but at least the poor animal will stay safe."

Téa took the thin rope Mother called a leash, looked at her brother who was sitting by a napping Bori, and dropped the rope neatly on his lap, "Here Nano, she'll be better off with you."

This time Nano didn't have to fight for his turn.

"I have to pay Mrs. Milagros her daily visit," Téa said.

The summer was in its last days of splendor, but the same couldn't be said for Mrs. Milagros' health or her company. Two of her nieces remained by her side, not to help, but to make sure she was 'well' taken care of.

Marina and Rosina, beautiful on the outside, but dark on the inside. They wished to stay as close as possible to their aunt's assets. They hoped to be there for their aunt's last breath.

Téa arrived and was almost sent away by the two jealous sisters. *Nice try*, Téa's face seemed to say as she slipped past the two and kept walking towards Mrs. Milagros' room.

"I don't like them," were the first words out of Téa's mouth.

Mrs. Milagros was in bed and was pleasantly surprised to see her favorite little person come through her bedroom door. "I'm glad to see you too...who don't you like child? Mmmm, let me guess...the two hyenas?" She said as she rearranged the pillows behind her back.

"Sorry but...Yep." Téa helped her with the pillows and then sat right by her side.

"Don't worry about it, I'm sure the feeling is mutual," Mrs. Milagros said still smiling.

"They tried to keep me from seeing you, did you know that? Why don't they like me? I haven't done anything to them...yet." Téa angrily punched the pillows around Mrs. Milagros. "I know I don't belong here, but..."

"But, what? The reality is, they don't like anyone, not even me. My husband's family are nothing but a bunch of greedy vultures." She paused to look at a small picture frame of her dead husband that rested on her night stand. "Those two hyenas know I'm on my last leg, and they are afraid they'll have to share with you."

"But I don't want anything." Téa looked confused.

"Well, I'm leaving you something; and not to change the subject, but wouldn't it be best if you went to some sort of school to better yourself?" The old lady looked at Téa.

"I think I will," Téa said when she saw the two sisters enter the room.

"I will? I will, what?" The old woman knew what Téa meant, but wanted to make sure. She had been wrong before when it came to her little friend.

"I will go to school." Heaven knows that wasn't easy for Téa, but she wanted to get back at the two sisters.

Mrs. Milagros took the news with grace and tried not to look too overjoyed, being careful not to scare the little bug away. Surprised, she placed her hands over her mouth in an attempt to cover her big smile, but her joy was more than her small hands could handle.

Almost afraid to ask, Mrs. Milagros said, "But, why the change of heart so suddenly? You must tell me." The girl waited for Mrs. Milagros' nieces to leave the room.

"I'm no good here," Téa said as her face hung low.

"What do you mean you're not good here? Of course you are. Now you're talking nonsense." Mrs. Milagros held the girl's chin up.

Téa began to cry. "I do nothing right, all I do is get in trouble and on top of that I almost caused my Bori to get killed," she sobbed.

"You? Kill that dog? I don't understand." Mrs. Milagros waited.

"Mother wants me to keep her on a leash at all times, but..." she paused to blow her nose with her white shirt; "I hate to see her like that, all tied up."

"Well, so what's the problem? You didn't try to choke her, did you?" Knowing Téa, the old woman was ready for anything.

"Oh no, quite the opposite. I let her loose so we could play chase, but instead to chasing the stick, she went after a rabbit..." It was very hard for Téa to tell the story and relive the nightmare again. "I called her, but she was too excited to obey my commands."

"I don't understand. Did the rabbit turn around and attacked her?" Mrs. Milagros asked.

The girl paused as she was about to answer and gave her a sassy look, "No! Really? When have you ever heard of a rabbit attacking a dog?" Téa quickly realized who she was speaking to and apologized, "I'm sorry Mrs. Milagros, I didn't mean to be so rude."

"Never mind, just finish..." The old lady was so intrigued that she dismissed Téa's gruffness.

"Bori ran after the stupid rabbit and didn't stop chasing her even after the thing disappeared down the rabbit hole. Bori was already inside the hole when I got there. All I could do was call her and dig after her. If it weren't for my brother, Diego, Bori would be dead now."

"Téa, that wasn't your fault," the old lady said with compassion.

"Yes, it was. My father couldn't get her out, and my brother felt so bad about it that he dug until he found her with his shovel. He almost cut Bori's leg off. She was lucky it wasn't her neck."

"Why don't you think it over? It's not a decision to be made lightly, and I hate to make preparations for nothing." Mrs. Milagros said somewhat harshly.

"No, I'd rather not. I've never been so sure of anything in my entire life." Téa was completely convinced that Bori would be better off with her far, far away.

"Very well then. Classes should begin sometime in mid-September. Be ready."

## CHAPTER TWENTY

# The Trip

Téa was having second thoughts about attending a school where the teachers were nuns, especially that far from her family. The only thing that kept her from voicing her thoughts were Bori and the knowledge that her aunt lived in the same town; Seville. Even that was not strong enough for her to keep her thoughts to herself. "Mother, I really don't want to go to that school. I promise you I'll stay away from Bori, or at least keep her on her leash." Téa's tummy burned with anxiety.

"Too late, Téa, this time you gave your word," Mrs. León said.

"No I didn't. I said I wouldn't change my mind," Téa clarified.

"Same thing, Téa."

"Mother, but it's so far away. I will die, I know I will." Téa felt nauseous.

"The only way you will die is if those nuns starve you to death, and we all know that's not going to happen. They are women of God Téa, just behave and you'll be fine." Téa's mother chuckled. Téa stood there trying to see the humor, but she couldn't. Mrs. León paused then added, "But then again, you're always hungry." She continued to laugh. Téa did too, but mockingly.

Mrs. León's laughter was her way of coping. She was very sad to let her youngest daughter go, but she felt it helped Téa to make the transition easier. She played it off so well that Téa believed her mother was actually happy to get rid of her.

Annoyed, Téa left while her mother prepared a cloth bag with a few things for the trip. Mrs. Milagros had informed her that Téa needn't take any clothes as the interns only wore the school uniform. Téa's mother was relieved since her daughter only owned two sets of clothes; the one she wore every day, and another one for special occasions. Once a week Téa would run around the house in her underwear while both sets were washed.

Mother and daughter waited outside for Mr. Luna, the chauffeur, to arrive driving his shiny black car. Both were nervous, but Mrs. León was increasingly showing signs of mourning as she fidgeted with her daughter's hair. To avoid tearing up, she looked down while ironing wrinkles off of Téa's clothes with her hands.

Téa pushed her mother's hands away. "Mother, please. I'm trying to watch for the car, and I can't see with you blocking my view."

Mrs. León normally would not have allowed back talk and would have put Téa in her place, but this morning was not the day to pick her battle. "If they don't come soon, your brother is going to wake up, and I'll be stuck with him crying over you."

"I wonder what's taking so long?" Téa asked, taking a few steps towards the direction the car should be coming from.

Mrs. León slowly walked behind the girl, paused for a moment, and said, "Let's go," and took the lead.

"But mother... what if they come?" Téa asked.

"Téa, if they are going the same way we're going, shouldn't we meet sooner or later?" she said smiling. Téa said nothing. "I know, it's too early for you to be thinking." Téa didn't smile back. Walking side by side, Téa looked at her dear Bori sadly. The poor animal had wrapped her leash around the tree she was tied to. She watched Téa walk away and whined and barked nonstop while wagging her tail so vigorously that pieces of bark were flying away like projectiles. Mother, with her unusually large hands, held her child in place with a strong grip on the shoulders, forcing her to keep on walking.

"Ouch! You are hurting me!" Téa tried to shake her shoulder free.

"I'm sorry dear, but I know you. I'm afraid that if I let you go you'll run to her, and believe me Téa, prolonging the goodbyes will only make things worse," her mother said; her voice softening along with her grip.

"I understand…" Téa tried to pull herself free and run away, but her mother was ready for her predictable behavior.

"Téa!" Mother shouted as she once again pinned her daughter.

"Mother!" Téa shouted back as a heavy tear slid down her cheek.

"Téa please don't make this more difficult than it has to be." Mrs. León fell to her knees while holding her daughter's face between her hands. She couldn't help but to cry with her. Téa opened her arms to embrace her mother, and for an instant they became one.

Mother and daughter walked away side by side, softly holding hands. Téa didn't look back. Not a word was spoken between the two, not even when they stopped at the iron gate. Mrs. León gave Téa a kiss, turned around and without saying goodbye, started to walk away. Téa knew it would be harder on her if her mother made a big deal of their good-bye, but it still pained her to watch her mother fade away without so much as a backwards glance.

Téa opened the gate but kept her eyes glued to the back of her retreating mother. Slowly she entered then closed the irongate behind her, Téa stood unmoved. She cried as quietly as she possibly could and for a moment thought of Bori.

With her mother out of sight, Téa dried her tears with both sleeves and calmly walked toward the end of her life as she knew it.

She saw the black car parked in the distance with the trunk open. As she walked past it, she thought it odd that it was still empty. The maid came out and welcomed her with the strangest of the smiles.

"Come, Mrs. Milagros is waiting for you."

Téa followed the maid in silence.

"Téa? Is that you?" Mrs. Milagros sounded weak.

"Yes, it is I!" Téa was surprised to find Mrs. Milagros still in bed and not looking well at all.

"What's wrong?" Téa's fake smile faded, and she couldn't help but have a spark of hope that there would be a possible delay.

"I'm not feeling well this morning my dear. Actually, I haven't been feeling all that great lately," Mrs. Milagros sighed.

"I'm so sorry you don't feel good Mrs. Milagros," Téa said tenderly as she sat by the old woman. "You know...I figure I don't need to go to school that bad...I can stay here with you and help you get better." Téa felt ill as Mrs. Milagros began to cough while nervously shaking her head no, even before Téa was done giving her proposal.

"Water?" Téa offered her a drink from a glass resting on the night stand. Mrs. Milagros nodded and paused to take a large drink.

Clearing her throat, Mrs. Milagros said, "Téa, as good as that sounds, I must put your interest before mine." Another cleansing cough made its way out.

"But..."

"But what, Téa. How long are we going to postpone your education..." the old woman held her hand towards the girl with the empty glass. "I don't want to be the bearer of bad news, but as you can see, my health is not getting any better," she said breathing with difficulty.

"And you are going to take me on a long trip as sick as you are? I don't think so...!" Téa responded as she set the glass down.

"Of course not my child, you are right about that. A trip like this one at my age and as sick as I am could send me to an early grave." Mrs. Milagros closed her eyes, and for a moment she looked dead.

"So, who's taking me?" Téa asked.

"Mr. Luna, my chauffeur, who else?" Mrs. Milagros' eyes opened to look at Téa.

"The poor man had to bring back in all the things that I might need for our trip after I decided not to go, but he should be done by now."

*Great,* Téa thought sarcastically.

"I'll come for a visit as soon as my old bones feel up to it." Téa just stood there.

"Téa, you're tiring out my poor aunt, and your ride is ready," said one of the hyenas as she stormed in. In reality, she had been right on the other side of the wall listening in since Téa arrived.

"She'll be on her way when I say so... if anyone is tiring me out, it's you," Mrs. Milagros said angrily.

"Of course dear Aunty..." Her niece smiled as she held her hands behind her back twisting her fingers with force.

"Don't call me that...as if you care about me. Leave us alone."

Scorned, she left the room.

Mrs. Milagros gestured for Téa to get closer, and when she did, the tired old lady whispered something in her ear, *"Beware of my two nieces...they are not here out of love and devotion for me...to tell you the truth, I think I must be near my end. Otherwise they wouldn't be taking my insults for this long."*

"Why don't you tell them to leave?" Téa asked.

"And end my only source of entertainment...nah!" the sick woman giggled a little. "Now, now go on. You need to be on your way." The old lady gently pushed her away.

Téa did as she was told, but before the girl lost sight of her old friend, she stopped at the door. For some reason she felt the urge to take one more look at her old benefactor, who was resting her eyes. Téa had a strong feeling, almost like a premonition, that she would not see her again. "Make us proud!" Mrs. Milagros said, sounding weak and tired. Téa nodded.

Téa had started the trip riding in the back as the maid had instructed. Mr. Luna was not very talkative until he heard Téa sobbing away. He stopped the car just so he could look at her. "It's going to be alright," he said as he gave her his neatly pressed handkerchief.

"But it's so clean...I'll ruin it," she cried as she held it with care.

"I don't care..." He waited. "Go ahead...make a mess," he said.

Téa hesitated before burying her wet face in the oversize handkerchief and blowing her nose into it a few times, forcefully and not too quietly, thanking him in between blows. Mr. Luna pushed the gas pedal. "Here," she said as she tapped his shoulders. "Thank you, I'm done."

His face scrunched up with disgust, "That's ok you keep it."

"Why don't you try to sleep some?" Mr. Luna advised her. Téa rested her head on the window. "Just try, you'll feel better," he said.

Téa was sad and exhausted from crying, yet didn't want to fall asleep. She liked Mr. Luna, but because she hardly knew him, she was nervous about being alone with him. After all, she was alone with a man who was practically a stranger and on such a long trip. Her mind wandered about the poor Mr. Luna. He had been nothing but nice to her, but she still couldn't wait to finally reach her destination.

Silence and fresh air pleasantly roamed the inside of the car. Téa had fallen asleep, and the chauffeur was thankful to have some peace. Nevermind, she was in the back seat; the awkwardness of having someone so young share his space, was something he wasn't used to.

She stretched, yawned and gave him an angry look, "Are we there yet?"

"Nope," he smiled. "Not even close."

"I'm hungry."

"Well, there is not a single cantina between here and our destination..."

"But I'm hungry!" Téa always awoke starving after a nap. Hunger made a little monster out of her.

"Just look out of the window and count the sunflowers," he sang.

"I don't want to count; I want something to eat damn it!"

"Hey, you're going to have to watch your mouth young lady, these nuns don't play."

Téa frowned and did as she was told.

The view was spectacular with kilometers and kilometers of yellow sunflowers making a carpet.

"Here." Mr. Luna grabbed a bag from his glove compartment. With one hand on the steering wheel, he passed the bag full of bocadillos back to Téa. "Eat!" She smiled.

"Thank you, Mr. Luna!" Téa recognized the bag. It was her mother's.

CHAPTER TWENTY-ONE

# The Runaway

"Téa...Téa, wake up. We're here..." Mr. Luna announced tiredly as he tugged at her shoulder.

The girl had fallen asleep again after consuming more than she should have. Aggravated, she opened her eyes halfway at Mr. Luna's insisting hand.

"Okay, fine... you can stop now... I'm awake!" The girl yawned and stretched.

The chauffeur left her in the car, but not before he too stretched his numb body. Thankful for the full moon, he was able to see where he was going. That, combined with the low gleams of a rusted light bulb, guided him to the main entrance.

Nose to nose with the large wooden door, he knocked, but nothing came from his poundings. He removed his gloves and proceeded to knock again, this time harder. He waited a few seconds before knocking at the door again. Still, no one answered. *I better get the girl ready.* Frustrated, he decided to go back to the car.

He turned around at the squeaking sound of the front door opening, quickly luring him back. Simultaneously, the head of an old nun peered out a few inches, just enough to show her eyes.

The old nun angrily blared out, "In the name of God, what could be so important that it couldn't wait until morning?"

The chauffeur turned his head to the car as he apologized, and signaled for Téa to come.

"I'm so sorry Reverend Mother," he said respectfully.

Then the old nun remembered, "You're bringing us Mrs. Milagros' girl."

"Yes, her name is Téa." He pointed down beside him and realized Téa was still in the car.

"Téa!" the chauffeur yelled.

The nun hushed him. "We didn't expect you at all, since this trip has been postponed before."

Irritated, the man went to check on Téa. "What could be taking her so long?" he mumbled. "You have got to be kidding...Téa come on...wake up..." he shook her.

"Hey...cut that out...I'm not asleep!" he jumped back.

"Then why are you ignoring me? You know this is it." He looked more sad than mad.

"I heard you! I just don't want to go..."

"And don't you think it's a little too late for that?" Mr. Luna had his hand open wide waiting for hers. With a sigh, she gave in.

Walking back, they looked more like father and daughter than a servant doing his job.

"Well, here she is..." the chauffeur said as he passed Téa's hand to the nun.

The poor girl had the chauffeur's hand in such a strong grip that it was hurting him. The no-nonsense nun broke the seal with a harsh tug. "You don't want to make it more difficult that it has to be, do you?" The chauffeur's eyes pierced the nun's with hatred.

"God bless you," the old nun said dryly as she dragged Téa inside, slamming the door on Mr. Luna.

The chauffeur felt uneasy and didn't leave right away. Confused, he stood staring at the door, but eventually managed to make himself walk back to his car. The troubled man sat in the car, lost in thought with both hands clenching the steering wheel. Even though he was just doing his job, he felt an overwhelming guilt for leaving Téa there. He shook his head and rapidly turned the ignition. *Damn it... It's too late to drive back.* He was exhausted.

Driving alone on the rural roads, the first few hours went by without incident, but as the dark of night came, it begged him to close his eyes and give into his dreams. His head felt heavy, and his eyes began to flicker. A bump in the road forced him to stop abruptly, realizing he had closed his eyes at the wheel for God knows how long. The poor man had almost wrecked the car into a tree. It was there that he turned off the ignition, lay back on his seat, and rested his eyes until morning.

The crowing of a rooster announced the imminent arrival of the first morning rays. Usually that's all it took to awake an entire village, however at Téa's new school, the girls had been up before the rooster even had a chance to open his beak. Everyone, that is, except Téa. She had just recently fallen asleep after a long night of sobbing.

The crispy cold air caused by her flapping sheets awakened the girl just as she was getting some much needed rest. A nun was waving them up and down to wake her up.

"Don't you know how to knock?" Téa said in between yawns.

"I did." The nun, younger than the last, answered her. "I also prayed over you, while you slept."

*It takes much more than a few prayers to get me out of bed.*

"Here, get dressed." The nun pointed to the uniform hanging on the hook behind the door. The uniform consisted of a white long sleeve shirt, a grey v-neck sweater and a dark blue skirt, brown leather shoes and white knee-high socks.

"You need to wash up. And don't leave your room without making your bed. I'll be waiting for you in the hall." Téa nodded and sighed with relief as soon as the nun disappeared.

She pulled the top covers of her bed somewhat tight, but left the white sheet exposed on the bottom. She quickly went to the small bathroom where a simple rust speckled tube and a hole in the floor served as a shower. Téa turned on the water, but nothing came out. She could hear the water slowly pumping through the pipes and then a cold blast exploded out. She knew she didn't have time to wait for the hot water to make it through, so she sprinkled her face, made sure her eyes were clean, and got dressed.

The young nun was where she said she would be. Sister Sara stood up and waited for Téa to come closer. "You forgot to comb your hair...and apparently to wash too," the nun said as she combed Téa's short sticky hair with her fingers. She quickly stopped.

"I don't own a comb. As you can see, I don't have much hair, and about the washing, there's no hot water or soap either," the girl explained.

"Follow me," the nun said calmly. "You'll get used to it," she added.

Téa stood not knowing what to say as the nun glided away. "I don't hear your footsteps..."

The young nun stopped in front of a large door while Téa, who had begun to run just to keep up, slid on the floor in a failed attempt to stop. Helplessly, she collapsed into a heap, her head pushing itself between the nun's legs, forcefully bumping it against the door. The young nun looked down at her tunic and the ball-like lump complaining of pain.

"Get out from under there..." this time she whispered frantically. "Do you want to get me in trouble..." The young nun had turned pale and was pulling Téa up from under her.

Téa shook her head; the nun straightened Téa's uniform. She knocked again, "Enter," Mother Superior said from the other side of the door.

"She sounds nice..." Téa said as Sister Sara hushed her.

"ENTER, I SAID..." Téa quickly realized that Mother Superior was not, indeed, nice. The door slowly creaked opened as the girl's head, red and sweaty, peeked in.

"And who are you? I've never seen you before," Mother Superior said while standing behind her desk.

Téa looked exactly like the other students. Mother Superior was expecting Mrs. Milagros' beneficiary to look more prim and proper.

"I apologize Reverend Mother, but this is Téa...Mrs. Milagros' beneficiary." The young nun was now standing behind the girl.

"What happened to your head?" Mother Superior asked as she noticed the bump. "Never mind! I don't want to know..." the old woman huffed as she returned her boney old body back to her chair.

"I bumped my..." she said feeling her bump with one hand.

"I repeat, I-do-not-want-to-know..." Mother Superior peevishly interrupted the girl. "Now, Sister

Sara...you are in charge of this girl. She is not to roam around, or so help me God you will be the one answering for it," she said without taking her eyes off Téa.

The young nun retreated towards the open door, unaware that Téa wasn't following her. The girl stared at the intimidating nun like a deer in headlights.

"Sister Sara, aren't you forgetting something?" Sister Sara came back for Téa. "Take her where she belongs, and for heaven's sake do something right for once, would you?"

Sister Sara grabbed Téa's arm and was pulling her as she ran. She was upset. "Are you taking me to class?" asked Téa trying to catch her breath.

"No, not today," she said as she slowed down. "I suppose I can show you around."

Téa didn't complain; it was her first day of school, and she didn't have to attend any boring classes.

"Where are you taking me first?" Téa decided she kind of liked Sister Sara, especially after meeting Mother Superior.

"What about our place of prayer?" she said as she place her arm around Téa's shoulder.

"That's okay, I don't go to church," Téa said.

"Do you pray at least?" Sister Sara seemed surprised.

"Nope, I don't do church, and I don't do prayers..." Téa paused, "I don't even know how."

"Well, then it is imperative that we go there first," Sister Sara puffed.

Mrs. Milagros had refrained from teaching her prayers. Téa was never able to recite a prayer completely on her own, no matter how many times Mrs. Milagros practiced with her. It was an absolute waste of time.

"Lady, you're wasting your time..." Téa yelled as Sister Sara unhesitatingly entered the capilla. Not wanting to be left alone, she followed her.

Téa decided to sit by her, and like a monkey copy everything Sister Sara did.

Before entering the pew, the nun knelt before God and made the sign of the cross on her chest, Téa did the same. The nun sat briefly, and Téa did as well, but when the nun leaned herself forward to kneel and pray, Téa didn't.

Téa was very sleepy and the capilla's peaceful atmosphere wasn't helping. The altar's burning candles, the aroma of incense, and the whispered prayers mixed with the occasional sound of Sister Sara's hand as she picked another bead from the rosary's endless string of beads, made it almost impossible to keep her eyes open.

A sudden uproar from the bell tower broke the peace with the announcement of lunch. Téa's body jerked, and so did the nun's.

"What's going on?" Téa asked.

"Lunch..." answered the nun.

"Oh, good! I'm hungry!" Téa sang.

Sister Sara made the sign of the cross as she stood up, and Téa joyfully did the same.

In the dining hall, Sister Sara showed Téa to her seat at a long table where other girls stood impatiently waiting for everyone to take their position.

"This is Téa!" the young nun announced to the group.

Everyone looked at Téa but said nothing. Téa looked behind her for Sister Sara, but she was already gone.

Nuns in aprons pushed a rolling table topped with a large steaming pot with a ladle on the side. As soon as each nun made it to the end of the long tables, the girls went crazy grabbing the plates and utensils that were placed in the center of the table. As chaotic as it was, they all managed to pass the full plates around until each girl had one.

Téa grabbed her spoon, but before she could dig in, the girl sitting on her right stopped her. "Don't!"

"Why?" Téa nagged.

"Where have you been?"

"Home..."

"Very funny, you have a home!" She laughed.

"In the name of the Father, the Son and the Holy Spirit..." Everyone froze at once, bowed their heads and held hands. The only sound in the room was the rhythmical voice of Mother Superior blessing the food with a prayer.

"Amen," she proclaimed after a long psalm. Everyone mirrored her *amen* in perfect unison, followed by the sign of the cross. For a brief second, there was silence, but as soon as Mother Superior shouted, "Let's eat!" there was a loud clanging of metal spoons.

Téa was the only one that after taking a spoonful of soup wasn't shoveling it in like the others.

"What's the matter? Why aren't you eating?" asked the same girl that earlier kept her from getting in trouble.

Téa didn't respond. All she did was stare at the lentil soup and compare it to her mother's delicious version.

"Do you mind?" The girl asked as she dragged Téa's soup bowl towards her.

"Go ahead, I think I lost my appetite..." she said while inspecting a tiny pebble that almost caused her to chip a tooth.

"Are you sure you want to do that?" the girl sitting on her left asked. "It's a long time until dinner, and they give you even less food, if you can call it that."

Indecisive, Téa shrugged her shoulders as she looked back at her plate, only to realize that it was already too late to change her mind. The hungry girl had polished hers off and was halfway finished with Téa's.

After the students were done with their meal, they were required to clean up after themselves and place their dishes in a large rolling tub by the kitchen.

Sister Sara was waiting for Téa by the dining hall door. Téa smiled, and the Sister smiled back. The nun resumed her duties with the new student, and it wasn't long until Téa was regretting her decision to fast. *Dinner is not going to come soon enough,* she thought as her tummy grumbled.

Finally dinner was announced, and served in the same manner, but the neighborly girl had been right; she was only served hot tea and a slice of white bread with a small drizzle of olive oil. Téa gobbled up the small meal in seconds, surprising the new girls she was sitting with.

"You're new...right?" one asked.

"Yeeep..." Téa answered with a hiccup. Every time she tried to talk, the annoying hiccup would sneak up on her, making them both laugh.

Once dinner was quickly consumed, the students had to attend the mandatory night mass before bed. This time she wasn't allowed to sit with Sister Sara.

Again, Téa mocked everyone's movements, hoping that her ignorance wasn't very obvious. Mass was over surprisingly fast, and Téa followed the crowd outside while looking for Sister Sara.

"Téa!" It was Sister Sara.

Téa turned toward the direction of the voice, running towards her as soon as she was spotted.

"Ready to spend another night in this Holy establishment?" the nun said as she placed her arm around Téa.

"Do I have a choice?" Téa complained.

"No," Sister Sara answered.

As they walked, Téa recognized the corridor and the bench where the Sister had been waiting on her earlier. Téa was looking forward to finally being alone and in her own room. Her excitement was short-lived when she felt the nun's hand pushing her away from the room.

"What...? Where are we going? Isn't this my room?" Téa sounded confused as the nun led her past the room she thought was hers.

They walked to the end of the corridor, and the nun stopped to open a small white iron gate that led to a large square patio that was succinctly simple. Téa was perplexed. It remind her of a correctional patio she once saw in a Boris Karloff movie.

Sister Sara was now waiting for her by a large round door. "Is this my new room?" Téa said as she got closer.

"Yes," Sister Sara said as she opened the door, letting the sound of the girls' brawling voices escape. Like magic all the noise disappeared when they noticed Sister Sara. Now you could hear a pin drop.

"Follow me," The nun said with a hint of sorrow in her voice.

Téa did, and soon she was wearing an ugly, long and rough tunic for pajamas and tucked into the smallest bed she had ever seen. It was also the hardest and most uncomfortable she had ever laid on. "Goodnight, God bless you," The nun said as she walked away.

Sister Sara turned off the light and closed the door behind her, leaving poor Téa feeling even worse than when she had arrived. Téa's belly hurt, from hunger and anxiety. For the very first time, Téa thought of praying.

CHAPTER TWENTY-TWO

T he deafening torment of a heavy bell being swung by a nun insisted that the girls come out of their sleep. Soon the girls were up and running with military precision. All of them washed their swollen faces with partially frozen water. One by one, they took turns. Each quickly poured a stream of water in the basin while catching it with the palm of their hands to rub the crust away. Téa was relieved that this was all the washing required, but was annoyed by the scampering of the other girls. No one complained, and she was not about to single herself out, at least not on the first day. Too confused to ask questions, she just did what everyone else did and followed the herd to what she thought was the dining hall. *Breakfast*, she smiled at the thought.

While in line, she looked for Sister Sara. She was distracted when an arm stopped her at the entrance, "Aren't you forgetting something?" one of the nuns said as she passed around the plates and glasses.

Téa took the utensils and followed the girl in front of her. A big bucket full of bread was waiting for each passing girl, but they were only to take one. In another line a barrel of buttermilk waited. The girls poured some into their small metal cups and went straight to their seats. Thankfully, Téa didn't start without any sort of prayer, at least she knew that much.

Téa was wondering when the nuns would begin parading around with their rolling soup pots. Everyone was talking about something, and it was hard to tell the various conversations apart. The two girls closest to her were having a not too friendly debate about something. One of them was pulling the other girl's hand away from her uniform pocket. "Give me half or else!" said the one trying to get her hand into the girl's pocket.

"Over my dead body!" she shouted as she tried to pull her pocket and its content away.

"If you don't, I'll give you some of this..." the bully swung her fist in a threating way.

"And you think I care? ...well, I don't! Go ahead, hit me if you dare!" she said clenching her mouth.

Afraid to butt in, Téa asked one of the girls, "Why are they arguing?"

The girl took her piece of bread from her plate and showed it to Téa, "This..."

"Are you kidding me?" Téa took her piece and gently placed it on the girl's plate. "Here, problem solved!" she said with pride.

The two girls froze. "A thank you would be..." Téa had not finished her sentence when Mother Superior started to bless the food, "Father, we thank you for this bread..."

It didn't take long for Téa to regret her generous gesture. That seemingly insignificant piece of bread was to be consumed with a small bowl of cold buttermilk, and that was all there was for breakfast.

Earlier, as they had stood in line, the girl who was behind Téa had taken advantage of the situation by taking an extra piece of bread while the nun was busy redirecting Téa.

"Amen..." everyone shouted.

"That buttermilk is not going to sit well in your stomach without bread," said the girl who had been defending her extra piece, and was now almost done breaking the last piece of the stale bread into the heavy milk.

"I had no idea that this was all there was going to be for breakfast..." Téa said while looking down at the thick milk. A hand placed a chunk of bread by her bowl. She looked up, and to her surprise, the same girl who had been fearlessly bullying the other one for the extra piece of bread, was sharing half of hers with Téa.

"Thanks!" Téa couldn't believe it.

"What class are you in? By the way, my name is Téa...I'm new," she said.

"I'm Matilde, and we are all in the same class," the girl answered without smiling.

"Really? Are the classrooms that big?" Matilde shook her head while the others ignored her.

The girl next to her whispered, "Here, it's a secret. There are two classes, and you belong in ours." She had never been this confused in her entire life.

A whistle filled the room. Each and every girl made sure to clean their place at the table, then stand in line as soon as they dumped their dirty dishes in the large buckets.

Téa wasn't done with her meal, but got rid of the leftovers since there was no more bread to dip into the nasty buttermilk. She tried to stay close to Matilde; somehow she trusted her.

"Where now?" Téa tugged on Matilde's sleeve. "I hope not to class?" She said as she tried to keep up with the nice bully.

"Well then, today's your lucky day…" Matilde said as she rolled up her sleeves.

In lines of two, the girls paraded across the school's big square as a few nuns watched them from afar.

Téa walked right by Matilde's side, separated only by a few inches. "I hope lunch is not as bad as yesterdays," she commented as her thoughts wandered around the delicious plates her mother lovingly prepared daily.

They walked past the school and entered the very back of the facility where rows of different vegetables grew. In the distance there was a long washstand covered by a tin roof. It was so large that it looked more like a shallow pool than a washtub.

As they came closer to the wash station, Téa noticed a large collection of bags overflowing with laundry resting on the ground. The girls who arrived first at the station didn't wait to start emptying the contents onto a thin but long, sorting table.

"What is this?" Téa asked.

"This is one of the classes you'll be attending until you pay for what you have done." Matilde's somber voice punched Téa to the core of all her fears.

"I don't understand; I haven't done anything...this must be a mistake..." Téa cried.

"Yes...we have heard that too many times...so don't waste your time driving us crazy...believe me, it's for your own good." Matilde sounded harsh, but deep inside felt sorry for Téa. "Come on, help me with these bags...there's nothing you can do now but to meet their expectations and make things easier for you and for us too."

Téa tried to pull a bag, but it was too heavy. Matilde and another girl took it from her and emptied it on the table, "Téa start sorting. Darks go with darks, and whites go with whites," Matilde instructed.

"Like this?" Téa grabbed the end of a bed sheet and shook it. Her face froze with panic when what looked like a bone danced through the air. "What the..." Téa fell backward trying to get away from the dust blustering in the air.

The other girls laughed at her. "You've never seen bones before?"

"You don't know where these bags come from do you?" Another one giggled.

"Where, from hell?"

Matilde helped her off the floor. "They come from all over the place, but mostly the hospice...the one you shook must have come from the graveyards, you know, they use them to empty out the crypts. The nuns took over the task of washing, mending and ironing for a fee," she explained.

"Yeah! Only, we do all the work and they...well, the money goes to those son of a bitches!" said one of the girls.

Téa shook the bone dust from her uniform and decided to keep her thoughts to herself.

"Come on over Téa...come." Téa wasn't moving fast enough. "I said come, someone has to show you how to do this..." Matilde pulled her by the arm. "May as well be me...or you could get us all in trouble."

Téa pulled her arm back and gave Matilde the only look she had, "Don't frown at me, I didn't make the rules..."

Téa kept her promise to keep quiet, did what she was told, and hope for things to get better.

The hours went by so very slowly. Somehow the soapy water and the scrubbing and washing of those garments made her feel remarkably close to her mother, who she missed more than she ever thought she could.

Téa's hands were wrinkled, but had never been cleaner. Her knuckles, red from the scrubbing, stood out in the soapy water. They looked like red dots floating in the sea of white sheets.

"Uhhh, it stings!" Téa cried as she licked one of her knuckles where the skin had torn loose and started to bleed.

"Here...let me see..." Matilde dried the injured finger and wrapped it with some old cloth she had in her pocket.

"Just tell one of the nuns that you need to use the bathroom and stay there for the rest of the shift. If they come looking for you, and they will...just tell them that you have the runs. They'll send you back to your room," Matilde said as she finished wrapping Téa's knuckles.

"But what if they don't believe me? I don't even have to go!" Téa was shaking with fear.

"I know, that's why you have to eat something that'll make you sick..."

"Sick? I don't want to get sick..." Téa interrupted.

"Just sick enough to give you the runs. Go grab some of those yellow flowers and eat the stem." The yellow flowers Matilde was referring to were 'vinagretas', wild vinaigrette flowers. She had used them for the same purpose, but now her stomach had grown used to them.

Téa rushed and picked as many as she could without raising suspicions.

She made it to the bathroom, but she was so afraid of getting caught that she began to munch them by the bunch; so fast that she almost gagged. To her surprise, they didn't taste that bad.

*All I need is to wait for the runs...* Téa thought.

Nothing was happening. She sat on the toilet and waited patiently for any signs of discomfort. "Come on...give me something...make some noise..." she whispered down to her tummy.

Impatiently she walked back and forth in front of the long row of toilets, stopping once in a while at the open door to take a peek with the stealth of a feline. Nothing, no nun and no runs.

Téa walked to the back end of the bathroom, leaned her head against the dirty window and stared at the open meadows through a clear space on the filthy glass. Two dogs were sniffing around in a very playful way. Téa couldn't help but to think of Bori.

"Are you done?" The nun's loud voice echoed through the bathroom's aisles.

Téa jumped, *if only I could squeeze through this window?* she thought as she tried to open it.

The dogs stared at her for a brief moment until one of them moved forward and peed on the yellow flowers, the other followed behind and did the same, trying to cover each other's marking.

Téa felt sick fast and began to vomit on the floor. The nun heard it at the other end of the toilet room. She didn't even bother to enter and quickly called some of the girls for help. Téa was soon rescued by Matilde and two other girls who carried her back to their room. Téa's green face was covered with bile, but a sickly wry smile gave her intentions away

## CHAPTER TWENTY-THREE

# Hurt, Hate, Hope

The first day of school did not go as Téa had hoped it would. Téa had always hated the thought of being stuck in a classroom, but now, as she looked at her hurting hands, she wished that's where she was.

Two days had passed since Téa ingested the wild flowers, and she was still in bed sick, wishing with all her heart to be elsewhere. Her stomach cramps made any other task seem like a walk in the park.

They had placed Téa in the same room where she had spent the first night. An old nun sat on a squeaky chair near her bed knitting with great speed. The girl was too sick to think about much, but somehow the constant clicking of the long wooden needles was soothing to her ears. Téa lay with her eyes closed, hoping to die rather than endure the agony. No such luck. The closest she came was when she passed out from exhaustion and slept for hours. She was awaked by the smell of rancid soap and to the sight of someone on their knees, their behind swinging from side to side, giving the floor a good scrubbing.

The old nun was still there. Téa felt better, but as she tried to get out of bed she almost fainted.

"Child, you are too weak to stand up," the old nun said. "Lord have mercy."

Immediately the old nun directed her eyes to the girl scrubbing and ordered her to bring a *tila*. Sweating and short of breath, the girl obeyed, taking the bucket with her.

"That should do it. A tila infusion will settle your stomach now that you haven't vomited for some time."

"There is nothing left in my stomach, not even bile," Téa agreed.

"Hopefully you're not contagious. At my age, whatever made you this sick could very well kill me." Téa just looked at her wrinkles and nodded.

"Aren't you afraid then?" Téa said feeling better.

"Afraid? Nonsense! I have been waiting all my life to be reunited with our Lord!" The old nun said it with such jubilee that it made Téa uncomfortable. "After all, we're not here to stay you know?"

"Well, I'm definitely not in a hurry to meet the Lord. At least not now that my pain seems to be gone," Téa said, gently rubbing her belly.

"What did you do to end up here?"

Téa's hand suddenly stopped. "Nothing..." she said.

"Hmmm..., help me understand. You ended up in this heaven because you're an angel...a fallen angel that is." She chuckled.

"No, I'm not an angel...but..."

"But what..." the old nun interrupted. "You are in this hell like half the girls in this school." The nun worked her needles faster than ever. "Once you learn your lesson, you can live in the other half of heaven. And believe me child, you're lucky that we're here to ensure that you learn that lesson. So erase the will for misbehaving; is that clear?" Someone knocked at the door. A different girl entered the room with a tray. The novice who left on the errand never came back.

The girl placed the tray on the night stand and without hesitation poured some in a cup. "Anything else, Sister Maria?" The old nun shook her head, "No, go in peace." Téa felt angry when she heard the phrase *go in peace*; such benevolent words did not fit their actions.

"Now, now...drink up." Téa obeyed, burning her lips with the first sip. "First lesson learned...you should blow when hot," the nun said.

"Bitch..." Téa whispered as the knot in her stomach came back.

"What did you say?" The old nun knew it was nothing nice but asked anyway.

"Bitter...it sure tastes bitter...may I have some honey?" the witty girl answered.

"No!" the nun said coldly as she went back to her chair.

Téa stared at the nun as she took her time opening a small bag and pulling out a black rosary. Neatly, she folded the pouch then placed it back into her pocket. The nun made the sign of the cross and began to pray. Eyes closed, her lips moved but made no sound.

*If I could learn to pray the rosary, maybe my luck would change,* Téa thought.

Téa watched as the nun lay the rosary on her lap and with one hand rotated the beads one at the time between her fingers. Every so often, she would whisper *Amen*, and her fingers would move to the next bead.

Téa worked her *tila,* sip by sip, having to blow a little less each time. Her stomach was genuinely feeling the benefits of the infusion. The nun sang her last *Amen*, made the sign of the cross and lovingly kissed her rosary. She then scooped it back into the small delicate silk bag and gave the bag a kiss too before returning it to her pocket.

Téa was paying close attention, while in her head debating whether or not it was a good idea to ask now or should she wait until the old nun had warmed up to her. She was hesitant, but couldn't help asking right away, "Is it difficult?"

"What, knitting?" Sister Maria replied already engaged in her needle work again.

"No, not knitting...the rosary, it seems very complicated."

"I suppose, like everything...only in the beginning. Time, patience and practice should do it; I believe ones faith will do the rest."

"Could you teach me?"

"Child...I don't have the time, nor the patience..."

"Pleeeease, aren't you the boss?" the girl begged.

"The boss? What made you think I am anything but a woman of God? There are no bosses here."

"What about Mother Superior, isn't she the boss?" Téa couldn't help but to be her usual self.

"Aren't you an insolent little girl?" interrupted the nun.

"Sorry. Sister Maria, I really want to learn." Sister Maria stared at Téa for a moment considering the girl's proposal.

"I can't take you out of your everyday chores..." the religious woman paused for a moment, "at least right away. Let me pray on it," she said as she grabbed her silk bag again. "I might be able to talk Mother Superior into transferring you to my sewing class."

"I hope so," Téa said.

"Now, Téa you need to learn humility and pray, because it's up to God, not up to your hopes. Understand?" Téa gave her a nod.

"I can see how your family lost patience with you. Now they expect us to teach you some sort of trade."

"With all due respect, not exactly. I was sent here to learn to read and write...but somehow all they want me to do here is...work..." Téa's face looked pale, and her stomach was hurting again.

"If my parents knew where Mrs. Milagros has placed me...I don't know..." Téa cried.

"Mrs. Milagros?" The old nun asked, "She has not...well, never mind."

The nun caught herself just in time and finished her thoughts in her head, *sent another of her charity cases. That explains why they moved this little girl from her privileged room to work instead of being schooled. Poor girl, she doesn't know.*

Sister Maria talked Mother Superior into accepting her plans. The wise old nun knew how to get to Mother's heart, money. She explained that there must be an explanation as to why Mrs. Milagros' family had a sudden change of heart regarding the child. It was just a matter of time until the family sorted the situation and they certainly didn't want the generous donations to stop.

Téa had been put in the private room away from the rest of the girls as a safety precaution. Finally she was given a clean bill of health and instructed to report to Sister Maria's sewing room. God is good.

## CHAPTER TWENTY-FOUR

# Unanswered Prayers

Téa pacticed her prayers with an old rosary that Sister Maria had given her. She constantly rolled the beads between her fingers with a single prayer, *to get the hell out of there*. The rest of her time was put to good use, learning the art of embroidery.

Meals were as bad as ever, but since her new chores weren't as demanding as the laundry, Téa was thankful for what she was given.

"Damn, how do they expect us to work so hard with just a small piece of stale bread and this dirty water they call soup?" one of the girls angrily complained. "We should be so lucky to land a job like

Téa..." Téa tried to ignore her, but the girl was persistent. She made sure she had Téa's attention by throwing a wet bread crumb at her.

"Would you leave me alone?" Téa shouted.

"That..." the girl stumbled.

"That what..." Téa saw the slim opportunity to defend herself. "That you wish you were in my place? Hmmm let me see, maybe you feel that you're more deserving perhaps...?" Téa was on fire. "Don't I eat the same crap as everyone else? Oh, wait...that only makes me qualified to take more crap." No one answered, not even the girl who started it all. "I'm sick and tired of all the nonsense with jealousy. We should stick together, not fight one another over some miserable scraps," she said while looking at the girl who stole the extra piece of bread on her first day at the school.

"Yes, that's right!" Matilde said backing up Téa.

Working in the sewing room was surprisingly stress free. She was surrounded by silence, except for the occasional singing of angelical voices to break the monotony of the day. Still, the girls had to maintain a certain number of garments, and the hand stitches had to be flawless, or the nuns would make them use their precious few free moments to fix even the smallest detail that only a master seamstress would notice. Many times Téa and the others would work well into the night where exhaustion and poor lighting made it very difficult to stay focused.

Téa had lost so much weight that not even her own mother would recognize her if she were to bump into her on the street.

"Téa, Mother Superior is expecting you," one of the nuns said as she passed her in the hall.

*What now?* Téa frowned.

Afraid of getting into deeper trouble, she turned around and ran towards the direction of Mother Superior's office. Having to skip through an ocean of girls would normally not be easy, but because of her slender physique, Téa had no problem sailing through. The poor girl had become so lean that she could almost float among the crowd.

Huffing and puffing she knocked on Mother Superior's open door, "Come in..."

*She sounds too calm.* Téa breathed as she timidly walked in.

"Mother Superior?"

"Why Sister Maria likes you is beyond my understanding, but she is not feeling well and wants you to keep her company..." Mother Superior dismissed her without another word. Téa stood there waiting for any further orders, but the nun remained quiet.

"Excuse me, Mother Superior?" Téa asked apologizing.

"Child...why are you still here?" The old nun answered, annoyed.

Almost stuttering, Téa asked, "Where is her room...?"

"Sister Teresa is waiting for you outside." Téa felt stupid and left Mother's sight as fast as she could.

Téa found the old nun in bed. She not only looked sick; she looked small. It was very surprising to Téa to see the nun without her black and white habit. A bad haircut made her white hair look like someone had resentfully glued cotton balls all over her scalp. Shivers ran through her body at the sight. For a moment Téa felt as if she were looking at herself in a mirror right after her painful encounter with father's scissors. Téa was speechless.

"There you are Téa, sit, sit by me child...are you hungry?" the old nun sounded tired.

*Am I hungry? Are you kidding?* Téa tried not to look anxious and remained calm.

"Here eat this. I hardly touched it."

"No, thank you." Téa said.

"What's the matter? Do you not want to eat after me?"

"No, that's not it at all!" Téa said.

"Then what is it?" Sister Maria didn't feel like talking; she just wanted to look at Téa. "You won't get in trouble, I won't miss it and neither will they. After all, it will probably end up in the trash."

Téa hesitated but she was too hungry to refuse the leftovers.

"Child, slow down, no one is going to take it away!" Téa had swallowed two of the three pieces of fish remarkably fast, bone and all, and was now cleaning the oily plate with a chunk of bread.

"Téa, put the tray outside of the door when you finish. That way no one will interrupt us." The girl did what she was told and gently closed the door behind her. A loud burp accidently escaped from her mouth as she took her seat. Téa covered her mouth with embarrassment, but the old nun only giggled.

"I'm sorry," Téa said, trying not to laugh.

"Dear Lord that was a healthy one." The nun grinned at Téa like only a mother could after watching her child finish a good meal.

"I believe you haven't burped that way since you left your home." Surprised beyond words, Téa stood in silence. "Don't you look at me that way, come and let me explain." Sister Maria patted her bed side in invitation. "Unfortunately there's nothing I can do. No one believes an old nun like me; trust me, I've tried," Sister Maria said as she wiped the tears from her eyes. "Perhaps you could?"

"Perhaps I could, what?" Téa didn't understand what she was asking.

"You could tell Mrs. Milagros? As influential as she is, I'm sure...no, I know she'll listen to you."

"Really, you want me to tell Mrs. Milagros? And how am I supposed to do that? Are you suggesting that I escape?" Téa thought it was almost sad, "Aren't you forgetting something? That lady cares for me and my well-being about as much as she cares for the dirt under her feet." Téa got up from the bed; her face was red hot. "She promised me the world, and here I am in hell!" Téa didn't care at that point if she was being disrespectful.

"Child, calm down, you must have faith. I'm sure she has no idea about your situation...there must be an explanation." Sister Maria looked deathly ill. "For now child, all we can do is pray."

The days went by and Sister Maria's health got worse, but she somehow seemed more alive than ever.

She busied herself telling Téa about her life. Normally Téa could have cared less, but the stories that the old nun shared were quite intriguing.

"How long have you been a nun?" Téa asked.

"Oh child, it's such a long story...I'm afraid I'd bore you to death."

"Well, I doubt that, and don't we have plenty of time?" Téa asked.

"Alright then, as you wish." The old nun began her story. "I grew up in an orphanage. As long as I can remember, nuns have been the only family I have ever known."

"So, that's why you became a nun..."

"No, they sure had a strong influence on me, but when you're young, at least with me, faith was secondary."

"But, you *are* a nun, right?" a surprised Téa interrupted.

"Well yes of course, but I haven't been a nun all of my life..." she chuckled. "This is not my first family."

"No?"

"No," the nun answered.

"My Mother Superior wanted me to leave the orphanage when my time was right and come back only if I felt the calling..."

"And when was that?"

"Well, I turned fourteen and a family hired me to be a part of their house help. I left the only home I had ever known and worked at the only thing I knew, cleaning." Téa was all ears. "I worked for a very affluent family for many years, even fell in love..." Sister Maria looked sad, but Téa didn't notice. "But things went terribly wrong when I was accused of something too horrible to reveal..."

"Not even to me...?" Téa asked.

"Especially to you...you're too young to understand." Téa frowned, disappointed.

"Is that why you came back?"

"More bread?" Sister Maria offered, and Téa took it.

"I came back, yes. But I didn't make my commitment right away...with a lot of prayer and the love of our merciful God, my calling came." Her face shone when she spoke of Him.

"How old were you when you finally became a nun?"

"I was twenty-one."

"I hope you don't expect me to become a nun."

"Only if you hear the calling my child!" Sister Maria went into a coughing spasm.

## CHAPTER TWENTY-FIVE

# Small World

"Are you really that sick? Téa asked.

"Why do you ask? Do I look like I'm getting better?" She smiled.

"I don't know, but sick people don't normally feel like having visitors, do they?"

"I don't know, but I can tell you one thing my little Téa, I breath better when you're around." Sister Maria pushed her food tray away, and Téa thanked her.

"That's it? You hardly touched your food. I hope you're not saving this for me! You need your strength."

"I want to share it with you Téa," the old nun rubbed Téa's hand. "I just have no appetite."

Téa was rapidly gaining her weight back, while Sister Maria's frame grew smaller with each passing day.

"Sister Maria, please tell me more about your life."

"Téa, I'm too tired." She slid down under the covers and turned on her side to face the girl. "This time...let's hear about yours...shall we?"

"Okay, but...is it alright if I eat while I talk?" The nun nodded. "Hmmm, I don't know where to start."

"Why don't you start with how you ended up in here?"

"If you're thinking that I end up here because I was bad, you're wrong," Téa said defensively.

"Really?"

"Yes, really...you have got to believe me!"

"Just tell me what happened..." the nun sighed.

"Okay, okay!" Téa took a sip of water before continuing. "It's true that I got in trouble once or twice, but not bad enough to end up in here, believe me."

"I believe you..."

"The landlady, you know, Mrs. Milagros... she pretended to care about me and wanted to teach me all about being a lady...because I'm no lady, right? I'm just a farm animal that she could do with what she likes," Téa said.

"I'm sure she did it with the best of intentions," the nun reassured her.

"Yes, just like everyone else... *we're doing this for your own good...*" Téa sang. "Bull..."

"Téa, everyone is not out there just to get you...I'm sure they have better things to do."

"Well, what if I tell you I was just a replacement for a daughter she abandoned hundreds of years ago!"

"What?"

"What...you think I'm making it up?"

"No, not at all...where?" asked Sister Maria.

"Where what?"

"Where did she leave her daughter behind?"

"She told me, but I can't remember the name," Téa said. "I know they had nuns too, but it was nothing like this place...no offense."

"None taken."

"I don't know why; it's not like I was going to replace her daughter... I guess it was just boredom. Rich people... I could put their bored asses to good use."

"Don't say that Téa...your youth can't let you see what is right in front of you...you should think before you talk..." The nun gave her a disapproving look as she shook her head.

Téa rolled her eyes and apologized before continuing, "But, one thing is true...It's all about her and making sure her last days on earth are put to good use..."

"And what is the use if I may ask?" Sister Maria asked.

"Going to heaven!" Téa said. Sister Maria laughed so hard she began to cough.

"Don't laugh. I know you're a woman of God and all, but you can't tell me that's not all old people think about; getting their ticket to heaven." Sister Maria coughed. "Who gives a damn about that? I know I don't. Once you're gone, you're gone." Téa waited until Sister Maria composed herself before continuing.

"I guess Mrs. Milagros was quite a hellion at some point, because she was involved in a romantic relationship with the gardener who worked for them."

"The gardener?"

"Well, the gardener's son...somehow she got pregnant...is there really a way to get pregnant without meaning to?" Téa paused to ask.

"I don't even know...just keep going..." Sister Maria had her hands over her mouth.

"Well, the thing is that when her mother found out about her daughter's pregnancy, she sent her with a nanny, before she began to show, to one of their summer houses."

"And?"

"I'm getting there, geez! Well, once there, she spent her time learning French and whatever else." Téa took another sip of water. "Everything was supposedly going well...until..." Téa was thirsty.

"Until...?" Curiosity was killing her.

"Until her nanny, I think...or maybe it was somebody else...ah yes, the nanny's daughter, told her all about what she heard her mother and the nanny discuss one night."

"And...what was that?"

"Her father wanted to get rid of the baby in a more permanent way...you know...kill it."

"Oh, for heaven's sake! The Lord have mercy on their souls!" Sister Maria exclaimed as she made the sign of the cross over her chest what seemed like a thousand times.

"I know! Who would want to kill their own flesh and blood? Animals!" exclaimed Téa. "Mrs. Milagros told me that thanks to that girl, and a terrible storm that blew through, they were able to keep the birth concealed. The nanny had to come up with an excuse, since she couldn't tell them that the baby had just disappeared into thin air."

"So what did she tell them?" The old nun had the look of a child anxious for more.

"That the baby was born dead," Téa simply said.

"So, I know you don't remember the name where she took her newborn, but keep going," Sister Maria said.

"Mrs. Milagros snuck her baby out in the middle of the night. I guess it was really cold and stormy she said. She felt lucky that she had made it. But she always wondered if her baby survived. Anyways, she found a torno, she placed her baby there, turned the wheel and here we are."

"In a torno?" Sister Maria asked.

"Yes, you know one of those..."

"I know what a torno is!" interrupted the nun. "Where was this orphanage?" The old nun sounded anxious. "Not many orphanages have one."

"Mrs. Milagros said that she planned to come back for her when the time was right, so she left a note in the basket pleading for the baby to keep the name she had given her."

"Obviously, for whatever reason, she never did..." the nun said. "What was the baby's name?"

"Oh yes, she never returned for the baby. Apparently her parents had arranged a marriage with a local businessman, and she couldn't shame her husband."

"Lord have mercy on their souls." The nun kept doing the sign of the cross over her chest.

"Ah, I remember now. She named her daughter after the orphanage, Vicenta something..." Téa couldn't remember the rest.

"Vicenta... de... Paul?" The old nun trembled, and she could hardly pronounce the name of the little girl.

"Yes! That's it! Vicenta de Paul! How did you know? Are you okay?" Sister Maria looked paler than ever. "Sister Maria...are you alright?" Téa was concerned. The old nun shook one hand as a sign for water while the other hand held her throat. Téa gave her a glass full of water and filled it again as soon as she was done.

"My Dear Lord! If this is not a sign then I don't know what is. Téa, I was the one who found her daughter inside the torno!" Sister Maria trembled and cried.

"What? You...? How...? Where is she now? That means I can go home! I need to find a way out of here!"

"All I know is that a nice middle-aged couple adopted her, but I don't know where they were from...I never asked. I was just happy for her...plus that information was classified." The nun took the glass of water and held it on her lap. "My Sweet Lord, my my my...!" Sister Maria said as she shook her head in disbelief.

## CHAPTER TWENTY-SIX

# Goodbye Kiss

Just when everything looked promising, Sister Maria's health took a turn for the worse. Mother Superior and a few of the nuns took turns keeping vigil over her. They all prayed, and for once in her life, so did Téa.

It was only because Sister Maria was a fighter that Téa was allowed to stick around, and she knew it. The poor girl held her friend's hand in prayer; her eyes begging her to stay.

Sister Maria signed for Mother Superior to come closer, and when she did, the dying nun whispered something to her. Everyone, including Mother Superior, left the room, everyone except Téa.

"Téa...don't cry...be happy for me." Téa tried, but couldn't.

*Happy? You are dying...* Téa's face shone with tears.

"What am I going to do without you?" Téa broke.

"You are not alone..." her breathing began to slow down painfully. "The Lord is with you..." Sister Maria's eyes were fixed on Téa. Her chest suddenly stopped moving as she took her last breath and exhaled. Sister Maria's dry silky lips opened just a little leaving a soft gap. That was it; she was now with the Lord, leaving behind a gruesome death mask as Téa's last memory of her friend. The girl sobbed.

Alerted by Téa's cries, Mother Superior busted in the door followed by her most trusted advisors. "Take the girl out; she is no longer needed," ordered the Mother Superior.

Téa stood up with the help of two nuns who escorted her out of the room like a piece of trash. Sister Sara was there to pick up the pieces of the sobbing girl. With a gentle push, the good nun helped her get up from the floor. As soon as she felt the nun's embrace, she broke down even more. "There, there...you knew this was going to happen. It is the inevitable circle of life. Pray with me for Sister Maria."

"What good is that going to do now? She's already dead!"

Side-by-side they walked in the direction of Téa's room. Sister Sara waited for Téa to open her door, "Rest, and don't worry. I'll be doing the praying for both of us." Téa said nothing, nor moved after Sister Sara softly shut the door behind her.

Téa stood staring at a large wooden rosary hanging over her bed. She walked slowly to sit on her bed. Lifting her arm, she jerked the crucifix. She began to cry furiously, quickly throwing the ornament across the room as she screamed an obscenity. The rosary broke and the crucifix flew in one direction and the beads rolled free throughout the small room.

*Oh Lord, I'm going to hell.* Téa got on her knees and quickly began to retrieve the pieces of the broken rosary. With the help of a napkin, she was able to gather most of them. Later she found some beads scattered across her bed and even under her pillow. Téa wrapped it all up, tied a knot with the loose ends, and then hid it under her mattress, hoping to come up with a believable reason for its disappearance. She lay in bed terrified of her own mortality.

*I don't want to die...* she cried. *I don't want my Bori to die... momma...momma...* she was inconsolable.

The next day Mother Superior ordered everything to go back to the way it was. Téa was moved back to the group room with the other girls and to her old regimen of clear soup and stale bread. Luckily her job in the embroidery room remained. Somehow it had reached Mother Superior that Téa had an excellent ability for detailed work.

*Why am I still here? Aren't you happy I pray enough Lord? Is there a reason bigger than me? If I'm going to die anyway Lord, why don't you take me now...* Téa had reached a desperate point in her life. She wanted to leave and wanted to leave now.

Six months came and went as slowly as a day without food and water. Energy ran low and Téa was back to her thinnest weight. She spent her breaks sitting alone under an old oak tree thinking about her family and Sister Maria. Eyes closed, she listened to the branch whisper to the breeze. As Téa breathed in the fresh air, she wondered what made people so mean. We all end up dead anyway, why not just be kind to each other. Téa caressed the fat trunk of the old tree and tried to hug it, wishing she could be one with it. *Lucky you,* she thought, *here you are, with no one messing with you...*

"Téa! Break's over! It's time to go back to work!" one of the nun's shouted.

Téa dragged herself up with one hand and with the other dried her tears.

Back at work, she neatly took her seat and sighed as she grabbed her needle work and began to do what she had learned to do so well. Stitch by stitch Téa became lost in her world. The other girls talked while they sewed, something about visitation rights. It rapidly caught Téa's attention, but as soon as she lifted her face with curiosity, one of the nuns reprimanded the girls for being chatterboxes.

"Girls, listen, if you have the need to open your mouth, it better be for prayer." The nun ended her sentence with an easy slap of her wooden ruler into the palm her hand.

"Did you say visitation rights?" Téa whispered to the girl sitting by her side.

"Are you praying Téa?" the nun asked as she turned around.

"Hail Mary, full of grace..." Téa began to recite her favorite prayer and everyone in the room joined in, including the nun. She prayed with all her heart to the Virgin Mary, *Please mother of God, let it be me, let it be me...*

At that very moment a nun opened the door and announced a visitor. It was for Téa.

Téa couldn't move; she couldn't believe her ears. Her prayers had been answered, and she couldn't move. Her body not only became feeble, but her mouth muted. She heard the nun ask her to leave several times but remained in her seat. The nun placed her hand on Téa's shoulder and tapped her once, which was enough to make her snap out of her chair.

Disoriented, she followed the nun to a place she had been many times before, the dining hall. There, two nuns waited. One guarded the door, while another supervised the conversations between the guests and the students; just in case they told more than they should.

Nervous with anticipation, Téa was ordered to sit at one of the large tables and wait.

"Téa...?" She heard her mother's voice, and her heart jumped. Her excitement quickly dissipated as soon as she turned her head.

"Téa, is that you?" It was her Aunt Sagrario, who looked nothing like Téa's mother, but had the exact same voice.

"Child, look at you! You look so tall!" Tita Sagrario hugged her for a long time. They kissed and sobbed with happiness.

"My little Téa ain't little anymore...goodness, you have lost weight my darling child. Don't they feed you here?" her aunt complained as she felt her niece's bones.

"Of course they do...Tita. I am just not as hungry as I used to be. We exercise a lot here, every day," Téa sang as the nun standing behind her Aunt watched her like a hawk.

After standing and staring at one another for a few minutes, they finally sat.

"How is everyone? Are they okay? How is Papa?" Téa wanted to know. She talked fast, afraid her aunt would disappear like a mirage.

"Relax, darling." She lovingly patted her niece's hands. "They are all well. Your mother worries about you, you know, as always. She begged me to come and check on you. So, here I am," her aunt said.

"Thank you Tita!"

"Well, I live close enough after all. I would have come earlier had I known that you were here."

"So, tell me. Why are you here? I know this must be against your will." Téa's face froze. "As much as you hate school, I mean!" Her aunt laughed.

"Ha, ha yeah...we all know how much I like school, right? As much as I love church." Her aunt chuckled as she thought that was even funnier, while Téa glanced nervously at the nun's piercing eyes.

They spent the entire visit making small talk, which was not like Téa, Her aunt became suspicious,

"Well, child, I think is about time for me to go," she said. "I'll tell your mother that you are alright, but I won't tell her how skinny you've gotten. She would pull you out of this school in a heartbeat."

"Yeah, ha, ha, why bother?" Téa half-heartedly giggled.

Watching her aunt being lead away by the watchdog, she realized her aunt was leaving and there was not a damn thing she could do about it.

"Tita...wait...I forgot to give you a kiss!" she shouted. Her aunt turned around and waited for her. "They are killing me here..." she whispered as she pretended to kiss her aunt's cheeks.

"What's going on there?" one of the nun's demanded to know.

"Excuse me! Since when is it against the law to kiss your niece goodbye?" Aunt Sarario shouted.

Finally, her aunt left and Téa was once again alone... but her eyes shown with a glimmer of hope.

CHAPTER TWENTY-SEVEN

# Heaven's Dream

Leaving hell was all Téa could think about.

She had been waiting anxiously for her aunt's return. After all, three weeks had passed, and she was still there.

Malnourishment brought weakness, and sadness had replaced hope. Her perky personality had succumbed to her misery. Now, to everyone's joy, she had become a lifeless body simply following directions without uttering so much as a single complaint.

"What's the matter? Are you crying?" A girl asked.

"No..." Téa sighed, "I have a cold." That was the nicest anyone had been in a long time.

"Well, clean your nose. It's making me sick," the girl complained.

"Don't look." Téa didn't care.

Téa walked away thankful that the day was almost over, hoping that maybe she would die in her sleep.

The girls retired to their rooms and after the mandatory prayers, pretended to sleep. Téa, despite her depression, found it easy to fall asleep. She dreamed her father stormed into the dorm screaming her name with an army of nuns dragging at his feet. It was one of those dreams that seemed so real that she actually felt her father grabbing her. In this particular dream she gleefully witnessed her father punching one of the nuns in the face as he shouted, "Forgive me Father!" Hearing her father's voice in her dream made her tear up. She missed him so much that she wouldn't even mind another haircut just to be home.

In her dream she even felt how she bounced around in her father's arms. The dream must have come to an end because everything around her turned dark as she was drawn into a deep sleep, so deep she couldn't wake up.

The truth of the matter was that Téa wasn't dreaming, and her deep sleep was her fainting.

Her aunt had returned for Téa, but the nuns had refused to let her go. Téa's mother and her sister had also come, and they too had been refused. Mother

Superior's excuse for forbidding the girl's release was that she needed Mrs. Milagros' consent.

That was the straw that broke the camels' back, Mrs. Milagros had been dead for a long time, and so a consent would be impossible, and Mother Superior knew that. Finally Téa's father, like a 'Toro de Miura' stormed through the school. He needed no consent. That student, as the nun's called her, was HIS daughter, and GOD and only GOD was mighty enough to stop him from taking her.

Téa succumbed to her weakness and for two full days and nights was unable to lift her eyes, not even the luring smell of the delicious stock that her mother always used to cure illness. It was a mix of meats and vegetables powerful enough to bring the dead back into the land of the living. If only she could take a few sips.

Nano couldn't wait to go back to the old days of sleeping with his sister, but not until the family doctor gave Téa a clean bill of health. Bori hid under her bed and no one could get the stubborn animal out of her room. Nano, with the excuse of retrieving his dog, stalled his visits until his mother would finally brush him away.

"Ma, why is Téa sleeping so much? I can't recognize her..." Nano cried.

"I know...those son of a bitches...if I had only known..." Téa's mother was too angry to cry.

"Mama...?" Téa said weakly.

"Téa?" Nano tried to jump on the bed, but his mother caught him just in time.

Téa's mother went quickly to check on her daughter and gently placed one hand on her daughter's forehead and with the other touched her own to compare temperatures. "No fever," her mother smiled.

"Nano, tell your sister to bring a bowl of *caldo*." Too excited to move, all he could manage was a stare, "Nano...? NANO!" Mother's benevolent hand reminded him of his task.

Mother glued herself to her daughter's side and with untiring dedication stroked her little girl's hair, apologizing every time her rough country hands rubbed her daughter's forehead. Téa would give her mother the best of her smiles each and every time. Mrs. León couldn't wait to bring her daughter back to the jubilant trouble-maker she once was. Téa grabbed her mother's hand, and in an attempt to show her that she didn't care how her hands felt, she began to kiss them all over. Téa cried with joy, and so did her mother. "Honey, don't...they're so rough...you'll scratch your face my darling."

"Here Mother..." Lola sang as she entered her sister's room.

"Stay with Téa...I need to pee..." Mother's face creased with worry, she gave her convalescing daughter a gentle squeeze on her shoulder before ceding her place to her older daughter.

"Nano, you're coming with me!" Mother commanded.

"But I don't have to pee...!" he protested.

Obviously she didn't trust that Nano would stay out of his sister's bed.

Lola, for once, had forgotten all their differences and lovingly helped her sister to sit up. "Come on, one more time..." Lola said as she helped. "Hungry?" Téa nodded.

Lola placed a large white napkin over her sister's neck and, careful not to spill the hot soup on Téa, began feeding her; but not before blowing on the spoon to cool it first. "Mmmmm...you like it? Téa nodded.

Halfway through the bowl, Téa was full. "You can't seriously be full?" Lola couldn't believe what had become of her sister's appetite.

"I'm tired," Téa said as she laid on her back and closed her eyes again.

"Here it comes, your favorite...Arroz con leche!" Téa's mother voice sang from the hall.

"Shhh..." Lola hushed her mother with her finger as soon as she entered the room. Mother stealthily left the rice pudding on the night stand. "Just in case," she whispered.

Lola and her mother backed out of the room, but just as Lola was about to close the door, Téa sat up and dug into the rice pudding. The two nursemaids smiled happily and tip-toed away from the room.

It didn't take long for Bori to come out from under the bed and start her usual begging. Normally, she would pick her up, but not this time. Téa couldn't compete with Bori's black glossy eyes and left her a little bit on the bottom of the bowl. Bori licked it happily as Téa burped loudly with contentment.

"Ah! Bori how I missed you my friend." Bori wagged her tail as she enthusiastically dug her face into the bowl.

"You didn't miss me?" Nano whined from the cracked opening of the door.

"Aaawww... Nano." She held her arms wide open, and her little brother ran to her. Her cheeks were starting to show some color. "Oh, Nano, I missed you so much..."

Nano clutched her frail body and wept. "Hush..." Téa lovingly whispered as she gently patted his back.

"Nano! What-are-you-doing-in-here? Didn't mama tell you to leave Téa alone? She needs rest!" Lola chastised as she stormed in.

"Lola...he's not hurting anything, and besides, I feel much better..." Lola shook her head and snapped the bowl away from Bori, leaving the poor animal licking the air. "How many times does Mama have to repeat that we are not to feed the dog on our dishes?"

Lola couldn't help but smile at the sight of the two of them frowning back at her, "Ah...who cares!" The three snuggled on top of the covers with Téa staring at the ceiling. "I never want to see Mrs. Milagros again!" Téa mumbled.

"You won't have to...she's dead..." Nano rapidly placed his little hand over his mouth, "Oops!"

"What? What did you say?" Téa asked.

"Nano?" Lola exclaimed. "Why?"

"Sorry!"

"Mama didn't want you to know until you felt better..."

Téa's thoughts swirled in her head. She began to think that maybe Mrs. Milagros wasn't so despicable and that maybe someone else had been behind all this.

CHAPTER TWENTY-EIGHT

# Where There's Smoke

"What's cooking?" Téa asked while she made herself comfortable at the kitchen table.

"Really Téa, you can't tell?" Mother answered.

"All I know is I'm hungry." Téa knew exactly what it was. "Can I have a taste? That might help refresh my memory."

"Here, have a taste. Your time spent in that horrible place must have altered your sense of smell," she said pushing a spoonful into her daughter's mouth.

"Bread, please." Téa took the spoon from her mother and while blowing on the green peas, thought about Sister Maria.

Alcauciles con chicharos. Green pea artichoke stew. The fusion of garlic, onions and white wine filled the air, making it hard not to gravitate towards the table. A basket of crispy bread waited in the middle. A tower of cheap white china waited by the hot pot. One artichoke per person floated in a sea of peas.

Before her school experience, Téa was the only one complaining about there being just one each; but now she was thankful, very thankful. Knowing there wasn't enough stew to satisfy everyone's appetite, mother had a bowl of fresh eggs waiting to be fried.

It had been a few months since Téa's father had rescued her, but she still woke up in the middle of the night in sweats, breathing fast, and her heart rapidly palpitating out of fear, only calming down when reality set in.

"Mother, someone is at the door, he's asking for papa..." Lola came in, milk money in hand.

"Tell him to come back later, your father is not due for at least three more hours."

"Mother, I would, but he looks official," Lola insisted.

"Very well then," she said turning down the flame on the gas stove.

"Lola, keep an eye on the peas," Lola nodded but didn't stay behind for long.

"Téa, look after the peas." Lola ordered.

"But..."

"But nothing...they better not burn or someone is going to get it!"

Téa was curious too but knew better than to let one of her favorite dishes go to waste. She could care less about her sister's threat. Téa took a piece of bread from the basket and looked after the beautiful peas.

"I need to speak with the man of the house," the young paralegal said. He looked disappointed.

"It must not be that important then, suit yourself," Mother said as she shook her head.

"I need to deliver this legal paper to..." he paused to read the next unscratched name and address on his long list. "It says here, Mr. Antonio León," he said as his accusatory finger pointed to her husband's name.

"I'm Mrs. León, you can leave it with me, or you can wait for my husband. He is not due for a while yet," she said.

"When is he due?" he asked impatiently.

"It varies...it could be just a couple of hours, but you never know with him."

The young man was wearing a well-worn, yet once elegant suit. He was in a hurry, so he opened his manila folder to an overflowing mess of official looking papers. Somehow he managed to find the one for Mr. León. Sensing Mrs. León's inability to understand the note, he began to read it for her. "It is a notarial order to be present at Mrs. Milagros' estate reading of the official Will, Monday, May 7th at 4 o'clock in the evening."

"It must be a mistake; we are not related," Téa's mother said as she pushed the note back to the young man.

"I'm just the messenger, señora," he said as he politely pushed it back to her. The young man wished her a good afternoon and left.

Mrs. León stood there staring at the back of the young messenger and his mended pants.

"Lola, read this." Her mother demanded as she entered the kitchen. Lola, out of breath, arrived in front of the stove with spoon in hand, just in time to pretend she had been there the entire time.

"Lola, are you deaf?" Téa said as she gently took the note from her mother's hands.

"I'll read it." Téa was proud of her new skill. She clumsily read the note, validating what her mother already knew.

"Well, it looks like we are going to be officially kicked out." Lola's remark didn't set well with Mother.

Téa had to help her sit as her feet threatened to give out from under her.

"You don't know that!" Téa exclaimed.

"Okay little miss don't know any better... I assure you that now that the witch is dead, everything is going to those two-faced good for nothing nieces. Mark my words!"

"Don't call her that!" Téa defended her benefactor. "Take it back!" She meant business.

Lola just ignored her little sister and nonchalantly turned her attention to the stove.

Mother tried hard to disguise her fears, but her teary eyes told another story. Nano stormed in pulling on Bori's leash.

"What's wrong?" Even he, who was always daydreaming, could sense the heaviness in the room.

"Shhhhh, It's nothing...don't worry about it..." Téa pushed her little brother back out.

Bori followed them with her leash dragging behind. "Nano, I have an idea. Let's go for a hike. I know of a place packed with chameleons." Nano's face lit up. She wanted to keep herself and her little brother busy with something beside worries.

Nano loved to watch the little reptiles do their magic... that's how he referred to the chameleon's ability to camouflage themselves over any surface you placed them, no matter how complicated the pattern.

Nano and Téa walked for a long time with Nano impatiently asking every few minutes, "Is this the bush?" The truth was, Téa didn't really know for sure where to look, because they could be everywhere and anywhere. Téa was still fragile from her sickness, and between the pressures of their visitor and trying to entertain Nano, she was becoming undone.

After a few minutes of looking for the evasive little magicians, they heard the familiar voice of one of the Varea brothers.

"Haha! Are you looking for one of these?!" Santi showed them the green chameleon, as he swung it in one hand.

"Put it down you fool, before you hurt him!" Nano shouted.

"Oh yeah, well stop me if you can!" he said playfully. "Hey Nano, check this out; he can fly!" he sang as he threw the reptile in the air, barely catching him by the tail. Poor Nano jumped up to try to save the flying lizard.

"Put it DOWN!" Santi's twin brother screamed from behind him.

Nano thought the animal would definitely end up crashing to the ground. Santi quickly grabbed the chameleon and placed it on his shirt. The chameleon clinched himself on the fabric, and Nano didn't think twice about taking it from him. "You heard him," Nano stuttered.

Téa turned red as she looked at Sam, he had grown taller and was now even more handsome than she remembered.

"What's wrong, Téa?" Santi sang. "Why are you turning red? Are you a chameleon now?" Santi's sarcasm rubbed Téa the wrong way.

"Leave her alone!" Sam slapped the back of his brother's head.

"Hey! What the hell?!" he yelled.

Sam sat on a tree stump, lit a cigarette, took a deep puff and like a pro exhaled the white smoke. Téa thought how much he resembled the hero characters of her films.

"I didn't know you smoked?" Téa said.

"Want one?"

"Sure..." Téa said as her little brother frowned at her.

"Here," he said as he lit hers. "Do you want to see something cool?" Sam said without taking his eyes off Téa for one second.

Téa took a puff and immediately began to cough dramatically, "This tastes nasty!" she exclaimed in between coughing spams.

Santi laughed at Téa, ridiculing her with mimics.

"Check this out..." Sam took the chameleon from Nano, ignoring his brother's goofiness.

"You're not going to hurt him, right?" Nano asked.

"Don't be silly Nano," Téa said in a reassuring tone.

"Yeah, Nano, don't be silly!" Santi echoed Téa's voice. Téa shot him an angry look and stuck her tongue out at Santi.

Sam was on his knees and was missing the silly little war the two were having above his head. Holding the chameleon's head in place, he gently pressed with his two fingers until the animal opened his mouth. Quickly, he took the cigarette from his lips and placed it in between the chameleon's clamped mouth. Like a mouse trap, the animal shut it, leaving the cigarette stuck between its lips.

"There," Sam calmly watched.

"Oh, great, now what?" Nano tried to take the cigarette from his animal friend.

"Just wait! You'll see!" Santi said as he stopped him. "He's ok."

The chameleon started to breathe the smoke and began to walk very slowly, tumbling slightly from side to side with the cigarette still trapped in his mouth. The poor thing began to turn gray and soon he was black. "Ha, ha, he looks drunk!" Santi shouted.

"Cigarettes should be smoked by stupid animals!" Téa and Nano were upset. She removed the cigarette from the chameleon's mouth and quickly put it between Santi's lips.

"Hey, I'm not the one who did it!" Santi whined as he gave Sam a look.

"Two for one! You both are equally stupid!" Téa pulled on her brother's arm and left without saying goodbye.

Nano broke away from his sister and ran back to grab the poor chameleon. The two brothers just stood there until Sam turned to his brother, giving Santi's head the back slap of his life

CHAPTER TWENTY-NINE

# Marina and Rosina

Monday, May 7th was near and uncertainty weighed down the León family, especially Téa's mother.

"Are you asleep?" Nano whispered to the back of his sister's head.

"Almost..." she lied. Téa had not been able to enjoy a decent night's sleep since returning from her nightmare.

"What's wrong now? If you want another back rub, you better fall asleep this time." Téa rolled her body over so she could face her little brother.

"Sis...are we going to be homeless?" Nano's whisper crumbled.

"No, of course not...we're here to stay." Téa caressed her brother's soft hair.

"I heard Lola talking with *you know who* about getting married." Nano was rolling his sister's hair with his pinky.

"Yep, but no time soon," Téa smiled back.

"She said that she will take me with her in case we lost our house...Téa are we losing our home?"

"Don't be silly, nothing is going to happen! If we have to move, you and I will stay together kiddo."

"But Téa, Lola's fiancé doesn't want you living with them... I don't want to be away from you again..." Nano sobbed.

"Shhhh, no one is going to keep you from me kiddo."

Téa held Nano in her arms and began to softly mumble the only lullaby she knew, hushing him with a reassuring *everything is gonna be okay* from time to time. Nano calmed down, but Téa kept humming until they both fell asleep.

The smell of coffee in the morning was never enough to pull Téa out of bed and today was no different. It wasn't just about being lazy; it was simply a heavy case of sleep deprivation. Nano on the other hand, couldn't resist the clinking of the spoon against the cup as his mother mixed sweet milk with coffee.

Mother waited to add the small pieces of bread. Migote is best served hot, and Nano was hungry.

"Good morning sleepy face." Mother said as Nano bumped into her. Téa didn't answer. She rubbed her eyes and slowly made her way to the bathroom.

"Bori stop begging," Mother said. Bori stood there wagging her tail. "Nano, you better not let her lick the bowl."

"But mom, it's just my bowl," he mumbled with a full mouth.

"No, it's not your bowl to give. Bori has her own bowl, and we have ours. If you keep it up, next time you will have to eat the migote from hers." Nano couldn't help but shake his entire body with disgust at the mere thought of eating from the slimy bowl.

Nano went back to his breakfast, trying to ignore Bori's insistent stares and impatient whining at the foot of his chair.

"Here have some," Nano poured some of his migote into Bori's bowl and placed it right by his side. "There!" He said proudly. Bori attacked the bowl and was finished before Nano could even pick up his spoon. She barked for more.

"See? It's never enough." Nano nodded at his mother's remark.

Nano positioned his leftovers dangerously close to the edge of the table and winked at Bori as he headed to his room. Soon, Nano heard his mother yell at Bori for dragging the bowl to the floor and breaking it into a million pieces.

"Oops! I think you're in trouble!" Téa sang as she returned from her long bathroom visit.

"Why? I'm all the way over here!" Nano shot back.

"Right, we all know you didn't do it. The bowl placed itself on the edge all on his own, right? I saw you dummy!"

"You're not telling Mom, are you?" Nano asked.

"Of course...NOT! Why would I do that? I have done worse than you have ever done, and you never gave me away...at least intentionally!" Téa giggled as she helped her brother button his shirt. Téa gave her brother a kiss on the cheek, and Nano wiped it off.

"You always do that!" Téa complained as she was getting dressed.

"Do what?" Nano asked.

"Wipe my kisses off!"

"It tickles," Nano said.

Téa gave him another one on the opposite cheek and tickled him, "Let's go!"

"Where?"

"I don't know, just out." Nano wiped his face again as soon as Téa looked away.

They were almost out the door when Mother stopped them, "Where are you two going in such a hurry?"

"To play..." Téa and Nano said in unison.

"Well, whatever it is you do, don't wander too far and don't get in trouble," Mother said. The two nodded and ran. "Téa, you forgot to eat breakfast!" Mother yelled.

"I'm not hungry!" she yelled back.

*Not hungry? That's a first,* Téa's mother shook her head.

"WAIT!" Mother yelled.

Téa pretended not to hear.

"You forgot Bori!" Mother had her tied up to keep her from walking on the broken bowl.

But Nano didn't, he was already running back to get Bori, who was anxiously trying to get loose and choking herself in her attempt.

"Keep Bori on her leash!" Mother said as Nano took her.

"I will, mother..." he said as he walked away, leash in hand.

Téa waited, "Come on!" she complained. Bori began to run when she heard Téa's command, dragging Nano with her on the sandy surface. "Let go of the leash!" Téa yelled. But Nano didn't. A dust trail was the only thing you could see from behind.

"What happened? Did you get tangled?" Téa said while lifting her little brother up.

"No," he said.

"No? And why didn't you let go then?" Téa asked.

"Mama said to keep Bori on her leash at all times...and that's what I did," Nano explained.

"Well dummy, not if it's going to kill you!" Téa softly shook the dust from his clothes.

"Really?"

"I think mama would rather kill Bori herself than let anything happen to you," Téa reassured.

"Don't say that."

"Well, Mama would never, ever, harm our Bori, but if she had to choose..." Téa took the leash from Nano. "Let's go, shall we?" Nano nodded.

Mother stood there watching from the distance. She couldn't breathe until she saw Nano walking unharmed.

*God, please keep my babies safe*, she prayed.

"Are you hurt?" Téa asked.

"No," Nano said, rubbing his wrist.

"Hey, I have an idea. Let's go to Mrs. Milagros' place. I heard mother say that there was a lot of throwing away going on!" Téa said.

"I don't think that's a good idea Téa." Nano stood there while his sister kept on walking.

"And why not...what are you afraid of? Just because the two stupid sisters told Mama she wasn't needed anymore? Besides, they won't see us. They never come outside." Téa stopped walking when she sensed her brother wasn't following her anymore. "Nano!" she called.

"I'm not going!" Nano said.

"Fine! Go ahead, stay there all by yourself! See if I care!" Téa walked away slowly, hoping her brother wasn't serious. He wasn't.

She only smiled, knowing her brother's pride would get in the way and make things worse if she rubbed it in.

Voices, barely perceivable were becoming clear as they got closer to the gate. Téa blocked her brother's way with her arm forcing him to stop, "Hush!" she whispered. Téa wanted a better view of who was talking, so like spies they stealthily drug their feet and crouched as they walked to the perfect spot from which to eavesdrop.

"Tomorrow, tomorrow is the day!" Rosina said.

Against Téa's predictions, the two sisters were out, walking side by side.

"Here, this one is packed!" Marina pulled from the empty basket as her sister daydreamed.

"Hey, careful you idiot! You almost pulled my arm out of its socket!" Rosina cried.

"Well, if you and your big mouth didn't have to dismiss the help, we wouldn't be here doing their job, would we?" Marina complained. "Plus, I'm not the one who must have fresh fruit at all times."

"You are a dumb ass, my dear. Why have the help around watching every move, listening to our private conversations?"

"Now, now...I think you're acting a bit paranoid, sister."

"Really? How come there's always one around when you least expect it?" Rosina interrupted.

"They're CLEANING!!!" Marina yelled.

"Don't scream at me, or I'll smack you!" Marina knew she was not bluffing. "You never know when or where you'll find one, supposedly "cleaning". They act as if they are working hard, but all they do is spy on us," Rosina explained.

"And may I ask... to whom they are going with all their findings? To our Aunt?" Marina chuckled.

"Yes, yes laugh all you want, but you shouldn't be so trusting, especially now."

"You think our aunt left something to us?" Marina asked.

"She better have!" Rosina mumbled angrily.

"She better?! And what are we going to do if she didn't...? I'm asking because killing her is out of the question." Marina cried out with sarcasm.

"You think you are so clever with your funny remarks. Just clean your face, and let me be." Rosina left her sister there alone with the empty basket.

"I'm not picking any...they're for you!" Rosina yelled at her sister.

Marina answered with a forearm jerk. "See if I share, bitch."

Nano pulled his sister's sleeve. He wanted to go home. Normally Téa would jerk back, ignoring her brother, but this time she didn't, "Yes, let's go. There's nothing here for us." She sounded sad.

They didn't have to wait long for the angry sister to finish her task. Marina put a few plums in her pocket and left the basket.

"Wait, I have an idea!" Téa said.

"Oh no, what now?"

"Come!" Téa pulled her brother with one hand and Bori with the other.

"Where are we going?" Nano asked even though he was being pulled inside of the castle's gates. "I want to go home!" he whined.

"We are taking mother a gift!" Téa said as she quickly began to pick plums.

"That's called stealing!"

"Nano shut up and help me!" Nano obeyed.

"I can't! They're too high for me!" he said as he jumped trying to grab some of the lower branches.

"And what do you two think you're doing?" They both recognized the unpleasant voice. Marina had come back for the basket.

"We are picking plums...so you don't have to!" the quick thinking Téa said. Nano was shaking his head no, but quickly began to nod yes to agree with his sister.

"Well, well and here I am thinking the worst. Fine, bring the basket to the back when you're finished." Marina seemed happy. "And don't expect payment...after all...aren't you doing this from the goodness of your heart?" Marina chuckled.

*"From-the-good-ness-of-your-heart!"* Téa mocked Marina's words as she went back to picking.

"Oh, and make sure the basket is full to the top!" Marina sang from afar.

"I have an idea..." Téa sang.

"Yeah, yeah, I love how your ideas always end up being my ideas too," Nano mumbled. "Well, I'm not helping you this time!" he shouted, sitting under one of the plum trees. Bori followed him and sat by his side.

"That's fine..." she wasn't mad. "You can't get to them anyway, just...just go home!" Téa ordered as she shined a plum on her shirt.

"Are you sure?" He got up and so did Bori.

"Adios!" Téa said as she gave her plum a bite. "Don't tell Mama a thing or else!" she reminded Nano.

Nano waved, glancing back at her as he left. He pulled Bori a few times when she tried to stay behind.

Téa decided to sit under a tree and give her sweet precious plum the proper attention it deserved. *Work is not for me,* Téa thought as she closed her eyes and allowed laziness and lethargy from a belly full of plums to set in. Suddenly she thought about her brother's safety, grabbed a few plums, and left. She had a premonition, and her stomach burned.

Running though the hills, Téa made it to her house, but her stomach burned. She wanted to throw up. The plums she once enjoyed where now giving her a hard time.

Storming through the front door she yelled for Nano. Nothing could prepare her for what she walked into. It was Nano. He had Bori on his lap, and he was crying, "Bori is dead...it's my fault...I had to let go!" Nano cried inconsolably.

Téa felt a sharp pain, first in her chest and then in her arm. She wanted to die. "Téa wake up! TÉA!" Marina yelled as she shook Téa's arm, "And that's what you call helping? You should be ashamed of yourself little lady!"

Téa was sweating and felt dizzy but as soon as she realized it was all a dream she breathed a sigh of relief. Finding the strength to get up, Téa wanted to thank Ms. Marina with a kiss. "You... what?" Marina thought Téa was going to hit her.

"Hey, relax...I was going to thank you!" Téa almost felt sorry for her.

Happy it was all in her head, Téa went back to work and began to pick plums with the energy of a lion. Marina stared at her, still in shock. *Bless her heart, this poor girl has lost her marbles,* Marina thought as she stood there.

Out of pity, Marina helped Téa pull the basketful to the back. Marina paid Téa with plums. She gave her a bag full of the delicious fruit, but Téa had eaten way too many and the sweet ripe scent emanating from the bag was enough to make her ill. But knowing her mother had taught her to never refuse a gift, no matter how ugly or how unpleasant, she said "Thank you."

CHAPTER THIRTY

# First Will Be Last

"Mr. Floran, please do come in."

Marina said as soon as she opened the large entrance door. "I'm so sorry you had to wait, but as you well know, my aunt's assets were automatically frozen with her passing." She gave the attorney a dry smile while he politely placed his hat and cane in Marina's hands. "Lord, it has been awful having to do without servants." The lawyer smiled back.

"Mr. Floran, may I take your coat as well?" She was nervous.

"Please," said the lawyer while quickly tugging an official looking envelope out of his inside pocket. "Is everyone here?" he said as he gave Ms. Marina his coat.

"Everyone?"

He did not answer. Mr. Floran's familiarity with Mrs. Milagros' mansion allowed him to find his way to the office. Marina followed closely behind.

Mr. Victor Floran, Attorney at Law, was born in Jerez de la Frontera and worked his way through his family's firm from the bottom up, because his father thought it necessary to build his character. He was an only child, and now a no-nonsense man, decent, generous and with strong ethics, unlike his ancestors who were well known in the region for being sharks.

Mr. Floran's father would often discuss his cases with his pregnant wife, giving their unborn child his first taste of the law while still in his mother's womb. She would caress her belly while nodding once in a while, pretending to pay attention.

Victor Floran was his mother's pride and joy. She cried endlessly when she had to endure the separation from her son during his long years at law school.

Mr. Floran, overweight, bald and unmarried, had grown a bold sense of humor which he often used to overcast his shyness. Being a severe stutterer in his youth prompted him to be a good listener and an even better lawyer. He lost his mother to a tragic accident just a few weeks shy of his graduation from law school, forcing him to finish early. Sadly the only ceremony he was able to attend was his mother's funeral. His father never remarried.

The lawyer made himself at home, sitting behind the ancient, but well preserved mahogany desk where he and Mrs. Milagros often took care of business. They always had coffee and pastries first before briefly discussing her finances. She had trusted him.

"Care for something to drink Mr. Floran? Water..."

"Yes, water is fine," he interrupted.

Rosina has been quietly listening to her sister's small talk from atop the large stairway. She tap danced all the way down as if she were Ginger Rogers; making it impossible for anyone to miss her grand entrance.

"I'm sorry it took me so long to get ready, how insensitive of me," Rosina's phoniness irritated her sister to no end. Ever since she was a child, Marina had been infatuated with her aunt's lawyer. It was undeniable that he had her heart. Blind to her sister's endless efforts to ridicule him, nothing could alter her feelings.

Floran quickly got up to shake her hand, knocking the bulky chair backwards. Thankfully the hefty bookshelf behind him bounced the chair back into its rightful position. Fearful of a sudden stutter, he cleared his throat and shook his head.

"Mr. Floran, please sit," Rosina said as she did the same with Marina by her side.

"Hmmm, Marina dear..." Rosina said with a disapproving look. "Aren't you forgetting something?" Marina had no idea what she meant. "The water..."

"The water?" she paused, "Oh, yes the water, the water for Mr. Floran!" she said, leaving the room at once.

"Oh, she has not been the same since our dear aunt left us. The poor thing has become...how should I say it..."

"Forgetful?" the lawyer said.

"Yes, yes that's it, forgetful." Mr. Floran dried his forehead. His constant perspiration regardless of the weather made his life miserable. A clandestine smile hid behind the open handkerchief. Ms. Rosina had always made an impression on him, teasing him about his inabilities with speech. Worried that his stuttering could show up uninvited at any moment, his comments were always kept to a minimum.

"Here's your water sir!" announced Marina as she entered the room with a small tray. She smoothly placed it on the big desk and poured the fresh water in a single glass.

"Why only one glass my dear?" Rosina asked. "There are three of us here you know?"

The lawyer thanked Ms. Marina for the water and quickly took a gulp.

"Mr. Floran, didn't you ask my sister if everyone was here?" Mr. Floran was still trying to satisfy his thirst.

Rosina realized she had revealed that she had been eavesdropping, "Well, at least that's what my sister said..." Marina swiftly turned her head to look at her sister. "Yes, when you were trying to situate yourself around the desk," Rosina warned her sister with a look in return.

"So, who's everyone Mr. Floran? We are the only family my aunt had, right?" Rosina was worried her precious inheritance was about to get complicated.

The lawyer poured more water into his glass, "Well, Ms. Rosina, unfortunately I can't tell you anything about the reading until everyone gets here," the lawyer said gently while Rosina stared at the red wax seal resting so perfectly on the white envelope.

"Someone should be at the door then, just in case," Marina said as she looked at her sister. "God knows I didn't mean for you to wait that long Mr. Floran," Marina said out loud, but her sister ignored her.

Rosina's eyes were still pinned on the envelope, and she wasn't paying attention to her sister's request. Marina understood that it was up to her to greet the newcomers.

Not knowing who could possibly be coming to the reading was not as bad as having to leave those two alone. It was killing her, and now more than ever Marina wished the help was back.

Marina opened the door hoping to find no one there, and most importantly wishing that it would stay that way. A knocking fist barely missed her face, "Oh, my Lord!" Mrs. León said breathing fast. "Are you alright Miss Marina? I almost hit your pretty face. I didn't expect the door to suddenly open just like that," Mrs. León said as she tried to compose herself.

For once in her life she was happy to see Mrs. León and Téa at the door and rapidly got the picture. *That's why these two are here. The help is part of the package.*

She pulled the two in. "Go to the kitchen and wait there until we need you," she demanded. "Oh, and pay attention to the door, we are expecting some important people." Mrs. León slowly shook her head as Ms. Marina walked away.

"Mother, what are we going to do?" Téa was worried.

"Wait... that's what we'll do," her mother responded.

Time passed slowly for everyone, but even more so for Téa who didn't know what to expect from her mother. "Mother let's go. Father is not here, and we don't need this," Téa begged.

Téa's father had not returned from work, and they couldn't risk being late.

"I have moved out of these people's way all of my damn life... I'll be damned if I'm going to let these two win, not this time, no sir." Téa's mother was gradually squeezing harder on her daughter's hand.

Before Téa could say anything, the service bell began to ring. Mrs. León didn't move, and Téa couldn't move no matter how hard she tried. "Mother, aren't we going to answer their call?" Téa said as she freed herself from her mother's grasp.

"No," she said softly.

"But, Mother!"

Téa's mother stood there as if in a trance. "I said NO!" she answered, this time harshly.

Meanwhile, perplexed, Rosina and the lawyer watched Marina lose her patience with the bell. "Are you out of your mind? Why are you calling the servants? Don't you remember? We-have-no-servants."

Rosina tried talking sense to her sister as she made her way towards her. Marina's rage grew with each tug.

"I-don't-un-der-stand!" Marina said in frustration as she gave an angry tug with each spoken syllable, the last one breaking the old rope in two. Marina ran furiously out of the room, screaming. The lawyer jumped out of his chair while Rosina acted as if she didn't notice her sister's madness.

"Aren't you going to check on your sister?" He asked nonchalantly. Getting no response and alarmed, the lawyer ran to investigate, leaving Rosina alone shaking her head no. Rosina finally snapped out of it and followed the lawyer to the kitchen where she found Mr. Floran restraining her sister as if she were a dog about to engage in a fevered hunt.

Rosina grabbed her bottom lip, pressed it together like she used to do when she was a young girl, and let go a deafening whistled, piercing enough to make everyone freeze. Taking advantage of the silence, she sighed heavily and calmly asked, "Can someone explain to me what's going on?"

Téa's mother was about to blow up again when the lawyer gallantly interrupted her by placing one hand on Mrs. León's shoulder and the other on her daughter's. "Mrs. Rosario and her daughter are the ones we were waiting for." Rosina stood in place smiling confusedly while Marina's face would have put a boiled crab to shame.

"I don't understand? What?" Marina giggled nervously.

"Don't be absurd! My aunt wouldn't do that to us...we are her only surviving heirs," Rosina sang nonchalantly as she tried to hang her hand on the lawyer's arm. He respectfully declined, and Rosina quickly left the kitchen scorned.

Mr. Floran remembered back to when during one of his visits, he offered Miss Rosina his arm; she reacted as if he had just told her a bad joke. Victor knew nothing had changed. He recognized her greedy attempt to have him on her side. Marina, still red, was satisfied to see her sister lose.

"Let's take care of business, shall we?" he said as he looked at Mrs. León.

"Please, Mrs. León, sit down." He gently guided the former maid with his open palm to the chair closest to the desk. Téa stood by her mother and nervously placed her hands behind her back shuffling her fingers together again and again.

Mr. Floran took a cleansing breath, and as if savoring the moment, took the gold letter opener that was resting on the tray and carefully snapped the document's red seal. The sisters repositioned themselves several times while never taking their eyes off the envelope. Unconsciously, Rosina puffed once in a while out of frustration while rapidly fanning herself. Marina just stared at him stoically. Mrs. León just sat there.

*This is the last will and testament of Mrs. Maria de los Milagros Alfonsa Eugenia de Soto of Jerez de la Frontera, province of Cadiz.* The lawyer's voice began to read Mrs. Milagros' last wishes.

*I appoint my attorney, Mr. Victor Floran, to be the sole executor of this will.* He read through the formalities of the document in hand, knowing that no one was really paying attention to that part.

*I bequeath my wordly possessions as given in the succeeding paragraphs, to my living natural successor, Vicenta de Paul, whereabouts unknown. I do this without any duress from anyone and in complete control of my senses.*

1. *My summer home in Algeciras will be placed in the possession of my beloved Catholic church to be utilized as a halfway house for unwed mothers and their children.*
2. *My primary residence in Jerez de la Frontera and my summer house in Chipiona will be used in the same manner.*

3. *All of these assets are to be returned to the rightful ownership of my daughter, Vicenta de Paul, once she is found, and a $10,000 reales reward will go to the person or persons that make possible the return of my beloved. Of course, an investigation will be conducted by my attorney to safely place all of my possessions in the rightful hands of my natural heir.*
4. *I leave the farm house, with 8 acres of surrounding land, to Mr. and Mrs. León for the duration of their lives, to be passed on to their daughter Téa León upon their death.*
5. *To Téa León I leave the party dress I had especially tailored for her, as well as the made to order photograph of us, as I know they both mean so much to her.*
6. *And finally, to my dear nieces Rosina and Marina, my two mahogany rocking chairs they seemed to enjoy so much, and all the art hanging on the walls of my Chipiona house to be placed in their care.* (They were all oil paintings of Mrs. Milagros and her family)

"And that is all of Mrs. Milagros' last wishes," Mr. Floran said. He closed the document and placed it in his shirt pocket.

"Well...we'll see about that!" Rosina jumped up angrily. "I should have known that you... my dear Mr. Floran..." She almost cried. "You sir, will be hearing from my lawyers!"

Mr. Floran stood there in silence and respectfully allowed her to vent. He opened one of the drawers and removed the key he needed to open a large dresser drawer. He made use of the key and retrieved the paperwork for Mrs. León. The dress was there too, but the photograph was pleasantly resting on Mrs. Milagros' desk, where it had sat since it was placed in the bulky frame.

"Mrs. León, I need your signature," the lawyer asked while the sisters stormed out of the house.

"Here, Mrs. León I need you to sign here," he repeated as he opened the document on the desk and pointed to the right spot.

Mrs. León looked at her daughter, and Téa knew why. "Mr. Floran, is it okay if I sign for her?"

"I'm afraid that's not possible little one." His stuttering had magically disappeared. "Well, Mrs. León. Can you draw a cross?" Mr. Floran asked as he helped her with the pen. She nodded and with the lawyer's help, did her best, "I'm going to need your husband's as well." She nodded again. "Have Mr. León come by my office anytime to take care of it. Alright?"

"I will Sir," she answered. "Thank you for everything. God Bless. You are a good man." He found her humbleness warming.

"No, God Bless you, Mrs. León. The world would be a better place if there were more people like you ma'am," The lawyer said as he gently held her hand. "Ah! I almost forgot..." The young man said as he struggled to get something out of his pocket. "This letter is for you Téa...wait a minute..." he hesitated, "You know how to read, right?"

"Yes, sir. I do!" she responded. "Thanks to Mrs. Milagros!" she added.

"Right, right. Well here then, it's all yours." Téa thanked him again.

The lawyer walked them to the door carrying Téa's heavy dress, which was in a tightly wrapped box. "Here I'll carry it," Téa's mother said.

A satisfied Mr. Floran watched as mother and daughter disappeared in the distance, and he was left behind with the intentions of locking Mrs. Milagros' home.

## CHAPTER THIRTY-ONE

# The Gift

Téa was looking for the perfect spot to read Mrs. Milagros' letter. Too many eyes made her nervous. Her small chest felt heavy, and the chance of crying in front of anyone was not going to happen. Behind the chicken pen felt just right; the only people who visit the solitary shack would not be collecting eggs, and could care less to bother staying if she were already there.

Téa held the letter in her hands, and for a while couldn't open it. All she could do was stare at the closed envelope. In a way, for her, reading Mrs. Milagros' letter after she was no longer with her was as if listening to her voice from beyond the grave. She thought about what her mother said to her while visiting the cemetery one day. *Téa don't be afraid of dead people, they are dead and the dead could never* harm anyone. It's the world of the living that you need to worry about.

Téa, smiling at her own thoughts, opened the letter. *Obviously my mother has never seen a Boris Karloff film.* Her eyes soon teared up at the sight of Mrs. Milagros' handwriting.

*My dear Téa,*

*If you are reading this letter, I have gone to be with the Lord. Don't cry for me, I am at peace with God's arrangement. As my mother always used to say, we are not here to stay. No one is.*

*As my health declines, and before I lose control of all my senses; I find it imperative that I prepare a new will. I know I never told you how much I loved you, but I'm telling you now. I loved you like a daughter; the daughter I had to painfully leave behind.*

*I see so much of myself in you when I was your age. I imagine I would have seen this in Vicenta. Carrying the hardship of my secret throughout my entire life inflicted my heart and my soul with unbearable sorrow. When God placed you in my life, I realized what He was trying to tell me. My pain became less, and my purpose became more clear.*

*As you undoubtedly know, the arrangement and partition of my estate has been taken care of.*

*There is nothing the hyenas can do about it now. I wish I could have seen their faces.*

*I wanted to keep you safe from harassment of any kind, and that's why not even my trustee knows what I'm about to tell you.*

*I wanted you to know why I was so insistent on keeping the dress and picture frame so close to me; it was for your protection, rather than my greediness.*

*I never wore jewels, but not because I didn't have them. My late husband showered me with them to try to compensate for his secret. Since I was never in love with him, I never really cared for them. Nevertheless, I understood their value. So, my beloved Téa, remember how you always complained about the heaviness of the dress? There is a reason behind it. I personally stitched most of my jewelry into the hem lines. They belong to you now.*

*As for that awful bulky picture frame holding our photograph, open it carefully as it has been packed tightly with bank notes. That and the jewels should be enough to comfortably take care of you and your family for as long as you live.*

*Téa be good, remember we are not here to stay.*

*God bless you.*

*Maria de los Milagros Alfonsa Eugenia de Soto*
The rays of the afternoon sun caressed Téa's face as tears ran down her cheek, some drops falling on the open letter. Téa shook them off, keeping the inked words safe from ruin. She closed the letter and carefully returned it to its envelope. Lost in her thoughts and with her eyes fixed on the horizon, she reflected on the harsh times spent in the school. Trying to recall a few good memories, Sister Maria came to mind. Sitting on the ground, her hands rhythmically dug the sand surrounding her. Téa felt the moistness coming from the deep hole. She held some close to her face and pressed hard. Like tears, the wet sand ran down her arm. *Thank you,* she cried.

In memory of my faithful companion
Miguel Goofy Goober McMullen.

The story is not over till the fat lady sings and right now she's busy writing *Mercedes de Nadie*, Book Three of the *Not Here To Stay* series.

BOOK THREE

# Mercedes de Nadie

CHAPTER ONE

# New Year's Eve

It was New Year's Eve, the night sky was clear, and even though it was freezing, nothing could stop the town's hunger for celebrating a new beginning. The streets overflowed with enchanting jubilee. Champagne bottles floated from hand to hand, and the excitement of the season accompanied their dancing and made the cold night inviting. The leftover generosity of Christmas was still flowing from glass to glass. It was the perfect time to wear elegant outfits and silly ones too. Wearing whimsical hats and blowing on non-musical paper trumpets, which would otherwise be considered annoying, felt just right. There was also the fearless singing, and the occasional friendly scream from one to another. This was the only time of the year when being drunk was a must. There were people everywhere, and the few cars that roamed the streets were hardly able to move, advancing only a few feet at a time. Partygoers that at any other time would come across as intimidating, were adamant to socialize with the people trying to drive. With the best of intentions, they tapped on the roof of the cars wishing to share a celebratory shot of booze.

Dorotea and her husband finished their dinner. It was her first time making acorn cream soup and a seafood boil. Her daughter Mercedes, who was six, had her first taste of clams and loved them. They left the dishes for later since Mercedes wanted to watch the festivities from the safety of their balcony. Dad wrapped his little angel in a warm blanket and held her over the rails. With a big smile, he showed his daughter the magic of the holidays. Dorotea watch them both with pride. She laughed at her daughter's face looking so red. *Maybe Felipe is holding her too tight*, she thought. Dorotea watched how her husband's breath floated away, as did her own, and noticed that her daughter's was not there. She realized something was wrong.

"Felipe, something is wrong!" her body trembled.

With the celebrations going full blast, he didn't hear her. She had to pull him in close and scream in his ear to let go of her daughter. When he saw his child's frantic look, he began to tap her on the back,

"Mercedes what's wrong? Say something, breathe!" he ordered.

"Oh my God Felipe, she can't! Open her mouth!" Felipe did but what he saw terrified him. His daughter's throat was swelling closed. Mercedes was wheezing and crying, which made things worse. Dorotea lost her composure and began to ramble throughout the house while Felipe grabbed his daughter and left with her in his arms. He knew she didn't have much time. His screaming wife followed him as he ran down the stairs. "She needs a doctor!" he yelled.

The three got into their car. The ignition was cold, so it took several tries before the engine turned over. Felipe was able to get out from where he was parked and onto the road, but as soon as he thought the people were going to let him pass, the car stopped. He was desperate to get through the tumultuous frenzy. Running over a bunch of drunks crossed his mind, but all he could do was yell and blow the horn. Unaware of the emergency, the people didn't move, and to make matters worse, everyone took it as if they wanted to party. In no time the rambunctious crowd was gathered around dancing, shaking the small car and rocking it from side to side. Inside the car Mercedes parents cried in desperation, but no one could see their tears. The windows were fogged, and their cries were mistaken for laughter. Their daughter was dying, and there was nothing they could do to help her. Little Mercedes took her last breath as the clock began to announce the New Year. Everyone jumped with excitement; some embraced in hugs, and some kissed on the mouth. In the center of all that, inside that little car, no one moved.

Visit carolinapmcmullen.com to learn more about Book Three Mercedes de Nadie and the rest of the Not Here to Stay series

www.ingramcontent.com/pod-product-compliance
Lightning Source LLC
Chambersburg PA
CBHW020148090426
42734CB00008B/742